# THE KINGFISHER

# SPACE

## ENCYCLOPEDIA

# THE KINGFISHER
# SPACE
## ENCYCLOPEDIA

Dr Mike Goldsmith

KINGFISHER

First published 2012 by Kingfisher
an imprint of Macmillan Children's Books
a division of Macmillan Publishers Limited
20 New Wharf Road, London N1 9RR
Basingstoke and Oxford
Associated companies throughout the world
www.panmacmillan.com

ISBN 978-0-7534-3321-8

Produced for Kingfisher by
Bender Richardson White, Uxbridge, England
Editor: Lionel Bender
Design and DTP: Ben White
Picture research and Administration: Kim Richardson
Proofreader: Laura Booth
Indexer: Sandra Shotter

1 3 5 7 9 8 6 4 2
1TR/1211/WKT/UNTD/140MA

A CIP catalogue record for this book is available from the British Library.

Printed in China

# Contents

# INTRODUCTION

The Universe – also known as the cosmos – is everything that there is, and ever was or will be. This book takes you on a journey through the Universe, from the telescopes used on Earth to study the night sky to the farthest reaches of space and time.

The book is divided into five chapters: **Chapter one** explains how the Universe looks from the Earth, and the ways that scientists (called astronomers) observe and examine it. **Chapter two** is about the Solar System – which includes the Sun, the Earth, seven other planets and a whole range of other objects, from moons to dust grains. **Chapter three** takes you beyond the Solar System to find out about stars and star-groups, such as binaries, clusters and galaxies. It also explains how stars form, change and eventually die. **Chapter four** describes how human beings have begun to explore the Universe, both in crewed spacecraft and by the use of space telescopes and space robots. **Chapter five** looks at the future of space exploration, at the amazing spacecraft and space colonies that may be built one day, and the marvels and mysteries that lie ahead.

# OBSERVING SPACE

Human beings have always been fascinated by the stars
and puzzled by them too. It has taken thousands of years
of study to understand them, and our place among them.
Today, amateur and highly trained professional
astronomers use an array of instruments and
equipment to continue this exploration.

# Watching the sky

If you ever get the chance to look at the night sky on a moonless, cloudless night, far from city lights, you might be amazed at what you see: a sky full of stars, together with occasional patches of misty light.

The human eye is amazing, but its use in astronomy is limited because of the vast distances involved. Over the last few centuries a whole range of devices have been invented to improve our view of the starry sky.

**Above: Observing space through a telescope**

## The sky at night

The brightest object in the night sky is the Moon. Its brightness makes it hard to see many stars. When it is not in view, more than 1,000 stars can be seen with the naked eye. Over a few nights, five of the star-like objects called planets (see Chapter 2) move around the starlit sky. There are also many small misty patches called nebulae (see p.86).

## Auroras

In the far northern and southern parts of the world, there are often bright coloured lights to be seen in the night sky. They are called the northern lights or *aurora borealis* – as shown below – in the north, and the southern lights or *aurora australis* in the south. They are caused by particles from the Sun crashing into Earth's magnetic field.

## Sky gods and the night sky

Before the development of science, many people believed that the things they saw in the sky were controlled by gods. More than 2,000 years ago, the ancient Greeks saw patterns of stars that they associated with animals and the legends of their gods.

# DAY AND NIGHT

WE LIVE ON A SPINNING PLANET. AS IT TURNS, THE SUN SHINES ON DIFFERENT PARTS OF IT. IT IS DAY ON THE PARTS OF THE WORLD ON WHICH THE SUN SHINES, WHILE ELSEWHERE IT IS NIGHT. THE LENGTHS OF DAYS AND NIGHTS VARY DEPENDING ON WHERE YOU LIVE AND THE TIME OF YEAR.

## PATHS OF THE SUN

Because the Earth spins, we see the Sun move across the sky. On the Equator, the Sun is seen above the horizon for 12 hours and disappears below it for another 12, and that pattern remains the same all year. In other parts of the world, the length of time the Sun is seen in the sky changes with the seasons (see pp.14–15).

**A:** The Sun's light is spread over a wide area so it is colder here. People living here see the Sun low in the sky, even at noon.
**B:** Sunlight is spread over a smaller area so it is warmer here. At noon, people living here see the Sun high in the sky.

North Pole

Equator

A

B

A

South Pole

**EARTH FACTS**
• The Northern Hemisphere is the half of the world north of the Equator
• The Southern Hemisphere is the half of the world south of the Equator
• The Equator is an imaginary line on Earth equal distance from the poles
• The North Pole is one end of the Earth's axis
• The South Pole is the other end of the Earth's axis
• The Earth's axis is the imaginary line around which the Earth spins
• The Arctic Circle is the southern limit of the 24-hour sunlit day
• The Antarctic Circle is the northern limit of the 24-hour sunlit day

North Pole

Arctic Circle

South Pole

Equator

Antarctic Circle

## THE MIDNIGHT SUN

On the Equator, the Sun passes directly overhead every day, and the weather is hot all year. If you go far north or south of the Equator, the Sun remains low in the sky all day, which is why it is colder there. The Earth spins at an angle to the Sun, so that at some times of year the Earth's North Pole leans towards the Sun. This means that northern parts of the world have long days and short nights. When it is midsummer in the Northern Hemisphere (which is in July), the days become so long in areas within the Arctic Circle that the Sun remains just above the horizon all night, even at midnight.

**Below: A long-exposure photograph showing the movement of the Sun in the sky during an Arctic summer's night.**

# The seasons

In parts of the world away from the Equator, the weather changes through the year, being colder in some months than in others. These different times of year are called seasons: summer is the hottest season and winter is the coldest.

In the Northern Hemisphere, winter begins on 20 or 21 December, which is the longest night and shortest day of the year. Spring begins when the night is as long as the day (20 or 21 March) and summer begins on the longest day and shortest night (20 or 21 June).

## What causes seasons?

We have seasons because the Earth's axis – the imaginary line that goes through the poles – is at an angle to the Sun. In July, the northern end of the axis leans towards the Sun while the southern end leans away from it. This means the Northern Hemisphere receives more sunlight at this time of year, so it is summer there. At that time, it is winter in the Southern Hemisphere.

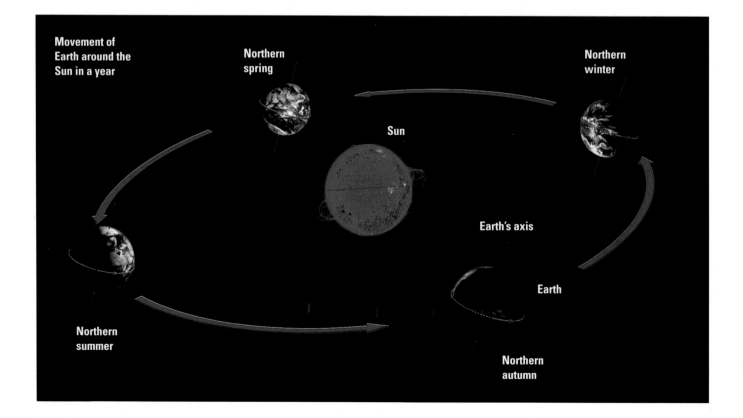

Movement of Earth around the Sun in a year

Northern spring

Northern winter

Sun

Earth's axis

Earth

Northern summer

Northern autumn

## Seasons and weather

Winter is cool partly because the days are short, so there is less time for the sunlight to warm things up. Also, the Sun is lower in the sky, which means its light and heat are spread over a wider area.

## Martian seasons

Earth is not the only planet with seasons. Mars also has an axis that is tilted at an angle to the Sun, which means that it has seasons, too. The effects of these seasons can be seen from Earth: when it is summer in the Northern Hemisphere of Mars, the polar ice cap (seen here) shrinks, while the southern ice cap grows.

## Animals in winter

Winter can be a difficult time for animals, because food is scarce. To cope with this, some birds and insects move to warmer areas ('migrate') for the winter months. Some other animals hibernate, which means they sleep for weeks or months at a time. Meanwhile, furry animals grow thicker coats to keep warm.

MYTHOLOGY

**PROSERPINA**
According to ancient Roman legends, Proserpina was kidnapped by Pluto, god of the underworld. Proserpina's mother Ceres was the goddess of the Earth. Ceres brought winter to the world until Pluto sent Proserpina back to her. Ceres then allowed spring to return. But Proserpina still had to go back to the underworld once a year; that is why winter returns every year.

# The turning sky

As the Earth spins on its axis, the starry sky turns overhead. At different times of night, some stars come into view while others slip below the horizon. They change throughout the year, too.

The collections of stars that can be observed in the night sky also depend on where you live. There are many stars that can only be seen from certain parts of the Earth.

## Polaris and the Southern Cross
If the Earth's axis was extended out into space, at one end it would pass close to a star called Polaris and at the other end to a constellation called the Southern Cross. Therefore, as the Earth turns, Polaris and the Southern Cross hardly move. Hence, they can be used to find north and south.

## Navigating by the stars
Because the stars that are visible change depending on both time and place, they can be used to work out the observer's position, by using clocks and star maps. This can be very useful at sea, where there are no landmarks to help.

## Seasonal stars
Stars near Polaris can be seen all year round in the Northern Hemisphere, but other stars can be seen only at certain times of the year. This is because the night side of the Earth faces different directions each season.

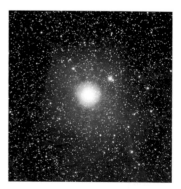

**Earth's axis**

**Imaginary Celestial Sphere ('celestial' means relating to the sky)**

**Sphere appears to rotate in the opposite direction to the Earth's spin**

## The Celestial Sphere

Although the stars are really at many different distances from Earth and do not go around it, it looks to us as if they are stuck on the inside of a rotating sphere, with the Earth at its centre. This imaginary sphere appears to turn from east to west, carrying the stars with it.

**ASTRONOMER**

### Tycho Brahe (1546–1601)

Tycho was a Danish astronomer whose observations of the stars and planets were the best that anyone had made up to the late 1500s. Tycho spent a long time studying, with the observations of hundreds of stars. His fellow astronomer Johannes Kepler used Tycho's observations to work out the laws that describe the movements of the planets.

# Constellations

For thousands of years, people have joined up the brightest stars in the sky to make patterns called constellations that resemble people, animals and things.

Today, constellations include all the stars around the main patterns that we see: every area of the night sky is part of one of 88 constellations.

## Constellations in space

It looks to us as if all the stars in a constellation are close together. But in most cases, some of them are very much farther from us than others are. They appear close only because they are in roughly the same direction from Earth.

Pegasus

Northern view

Southern view

Phoenix

Crux (Southern Cross)

Libra

Scorpio

Hercules

Ursa Major

Leo

Plane of
Earth's
Equator

Earth's axis

Celestial Sphere

## The ecliptic

As you walk around a tree, its background changes. In the same way, as the Earth goes around the Sun, its background of stars changes. To us, it looks like the Sun moves gradually around the Celestial Sphere every year. The path it takes is called the ecliptic. The ecliptic passes through all the zodiac constellations.

**The 12 signs of the zodiac are:**

| | | |
|---|---|---|
| 1. Capricorn | 5. Taurus | 9. Virgo |
| 2. Aquarius | 6. Gemini | 10. Libra |
| 3. Pisces | 7. Cancer | 11. Scorpio |
| 4. Aries | 8. Leo | 12. Sagittarius |

During the Renaissance – the rebirth of science from around 1400 to 1600 – many artists created images of the night sky showing some of the signs of the zodiac.

## The zodiac

Although we cannot usually see constellations during the day, they are still there in the sky, and the Sun passes in front of 12 of them during the year. These 12 constellations are called the signs of the zodiac and have been used for many centuries for fortune-telling. Many of the zodiac constellations are animals, and the Greek word *zodiac* means 'circle of animals' in English.

MYTHOLOGY

**ORION LEGENDS AND MYTHS**

There are legends about the constellation of Orion in many cultures. In ancient Greece, he was a mythical hunter whom the god Zeus placed in the heavens, while the Khoisan people of Africa think of the three stars in Orion's belt as being three zebras. In Japan, the stars are said to form the shape of a traditional drum called a *tsuzumi*.

# Eclipses

In an eclipse, a planet or moon blocks light from a star. In a solar eclipse, the Moon blocks sunlight. In a lunar eclipse, Earth blocks sunlight.

Many ancient civilizations regarded eclipses as signs that terrible events would occur. Today, we know that the explanation for them is simple: solar eclipses happen when the Moon's shadow falls on the Earth, and lunar eclipses when the Earth's shadow falls on the Moon.

**USEFUL ECLIPSES**
Eclipses are useful as well as exciting. During a solar eclipse, the Sun's outer atmosphere, called the corona, can be seen and studied – usually it is lost in the glare of the Sun. And, when people in history mention eclipses, their writings can be dated exactly because astronomers know when every historical eclipse took place.

## World of eclipses

The Earth is the only planet from which a total solar eclipse can be seen. This is because our Moon happens to be about 400 times smaller than the Sun and also about 400 times closer to us. So the sizes of the Sun and Moon in the sky are almost the same. Because of this, the Moon can just cover the Sun during an eclipse.

Moon   Sun
Earth

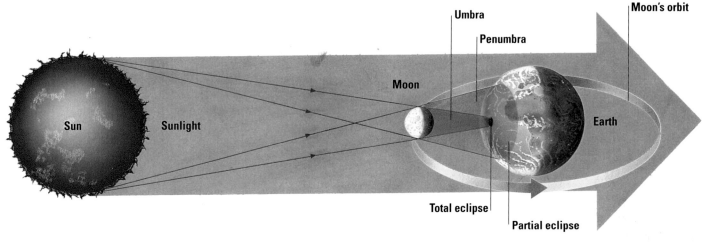

Labels on diagram: Umbra, Penumbra, Moon's orbit, Moon, Earth, Sun, Sunlight, Total eclipse, Partial eclipse

## Solar eclipses

Solar eclipses can be seen only from those parts of the Earth where the Moon's shadow falls. People in the so-called 'umbra' see a total eclipse because the Sun is completely covered by the Moon, while those in the 'penumbra' see just part of the Sun blacked out: a partial eclipse.

## Eclipses on other planets

Although total solar eclipses happen only on Earth, partial ones can be seen from many planets. This is an eclipse of the Sun by the Martian moon Phobos, as seen by the Mars rover *Opportunity*.

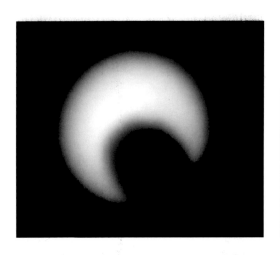

## Lunar eclipses

Lunar eclipses happen more often than solar ones and can be seen from anywhere on Earth that the Moon is visible. The Moon turns red during a lunar eclipse. This is because, although the Earth's shadow cuts off direct sunlight from the Moon, some red light from the Sun is bent towards the Moon by our atmosphere. Like solar eclipses, lunar eclipses can be either partial or total.

## Powers of the eclipse

It is said that Columbus's knowledge of an upcoming lunar eclipse in 1504 was a life-saver. When he fell out with some Jamaican islanders who refused his crew food and water, Columbus claimed he had power over the Moon and threatened to remove it from the sky. When the islanders still refused, the Moon began to vanish, only returning when Columbus ordered it to – by which time the worried islanders had provided the supplies.

# RADIATION FROM SPACE

LIGHT IS JUST ONE OF MANY TYPES OF RADIATION THAT THE SUN, STARS AND OTHER OBJECTS SEND OUT INTO SPACE. ALTHOUGH WE CANNOT SEE THE OTHER KINDS, THERE ARE INSTRUMENTS THAT CAN DETECT THEM AND MAKE MAPS AND PICTURES FOR US.

## USING RADIATION

We use different types of radiation for different things. This diagram shows some of them:

• Long-wavelength radio waves are used for radio broadcasts.

• Shorter radio waves are used for TV broadcasts.

• Very short radio waves are used in radar systems.

• The shortest radio waves, also called microwaves, are used to cook food.

• Infrared waves are used in sensors and remote controls.

• Visible light allows us to see.

• Sunbeds use ultraviolet radiation.

• X-rays allow us to look inside the body.

• Gamma rays are so powerful that they can look inside metal objects such as jet engines.

## THE ELECTROMAGNETIC SPECTRUM

The electromagnetic spectrum includes all the different types of radiation, including visible light. All radiation travels as if it is made of waves. The different types of radiation differ according to the lengths of their waves. Radio waves have the longest waves, then infrared, followed by visible light, ultraviolet, X-rays and gamma rays. The shorter the wavelength of radiation, the more powerful it can be.

Television

Radio

## THE VISIBLE SPECTRUM

White light is made of various colours of light. We can see this when raindrops split white sunlight into colours to make a rainbow. The colours in a rainbow are arranged in the order of their wavelengths from long-wavelength red light to short-wavelength violet light.

Visible spectrum

Gamma-ray image of a jet engine

X-ray image of a hand

Ultraviolet sunbed

Human eye (can only detect visible light)

Infrared sensor

Microwave oven

Radar aerial

## HEAT RAYS

A prism is a piece of glass that breaks up light into its spectrum of colours. The astronomer William Herschel (1738–1822) used a prism to make a spectrum of sunlight and then placed a thermometer just beyond the red end. The thermometer indicated that heat was present: Herschel had discovered invisible infrared radiation.

## LINE SPECTRA

Sometimes, when light from an object in space is spread out, it does not make a broad band of colour like a rainbow. Instead, groups of coloured lines appear. These are called spectral lines and can tell astronomers what the object is made of, how hot it is, how fast it is moving and even how strong its magnetic field is.

# Optical telescopes

The majority of the objects that astronomers look at are very dim – too dim to be seen with the naked eye. Optical telescopes make these objects look closer and brighter.

To capture as much light as possible, the best telescopes use huge mirrors or pieces of shaped glass called lenses. These are made very carefully so they are extremely smooth and have exactly the right shape.

## What is a telescope?

A telescope is an instrument for viewing distant objects. A good optical telescope needs a well-made primary (main) lens or mirror and a special camera or other device to make an image or measurements of the objects it studies. Electric motors are used to move and point the telescope in the right direction and then to keep it moving slowly at exactly the right speed, so that it keeps up with the stars as the sky turns.

### EARLY TELESCOPES

**1609**
First astronomical telescope, built by Galileo Galilei

**1688**
First reflector, built by Sir Isaac Newton

**1845**
Largest telescope for over 50 years, 1.83m across. Built by William Parsons (Lord Rosse)

## Herschel's telescope

The astronomer William Herschel built more than 400 telescopes. The one below had a mirror 1.26m across, and the first time he used it he discovered a new moon of Saturn.

**William's sister Caroline helped him to observe the stars and planets.**

**Right: A laser is used to make a target high in the sky for telescopes to focus on.**

## Refractors

Refractors are telescopes that use lenses to gather light. They are tougher than reflectors (see below) and are often used by amateur astronomers, but the lenses are very heavy: if they are more than about one metre across, they sag under their own weight.

Light rays

Object lens

Eyepiece

## Giant telescope

The Hale telescope at Palomar Observatory in the USA is a reflector (see below) – it has a mirror 5.1m across. It was built in 1948 and was the largest telescope in the world for the next 28 years. It is still in use today.

Horseshoe-shaped mount allows telescope to point at any part of the sky

## Reflectors

All the world's largest telescopes are reflectors, which use a curved mirror to capture light. A secondary mirror sends the light to a smaller lens called an eyepiece. The eyepiece focuses the light onto the eye or recording instrument.

Light rays

Object mirror

Eyepiece

Secondary mirror

# Radio telescopes

The Universe is full of radio waves, but people discovered them only in 1887, and radio astronomy did not begin until 1932.

Because radio waves are so long, the instruments that detect them have to be large. Even a small radio-telescope dish is larger than the primary lens or mirror of an optical telescope.

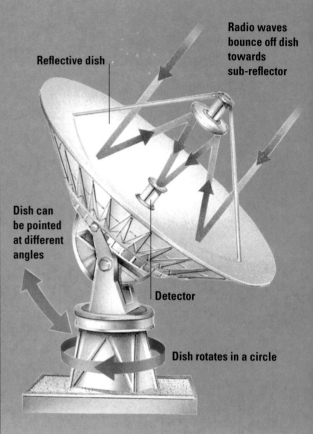

**Reflective dish**

**Radio waves bounce off dish towards sub-reflector**

**Dish can be pointed at different angles**

**Detector**

**Dish rotates in a circle**

## How radio telescopes work

The dish of a radio telescope is designed so that radio waves are reflected by it to a single point above the disc's centre, called the focus. A sub-reflector at this point picks up the radio waves and sends them to a detector. Then they are amplified, or made stronger.

### Arrays

Rather than making one huge radio telescope, it is often easier to make several of them point at the same object and join all the results together. This is called an array.

## Linking telescopes

Earth-rotation synthesis is a way of making arrays of radio telescopes work together even better. If they all point at the same object in the sky for many hours, the turning of the Earth means that they each provide a range of views from different points. Using computers, the views are combined to produce an improved image.

## Radio windows

Most radio waves (shown above as blue) travel through the atmosphere as easily as light rays (multicoloured). The only radio waves that do not pass through are either very short, or longer than 100m (purple). A layer in the atmosphere called the ionosphere stops these waves. The ionosphere is useful to us because it can be used to bounce our own radio messages from one part of the Earth to another.

## Accidental astronomer

Karl Jansky (1905–1950) became the first radio astronomer when he detected radio waves from the Milky Way (see pp.88-89) in 1931. He was looking for sources of noise called static that interfered with radio broadcasts, using a radio detector which he had constructed. It could be turned, which helped to pinpoint the sources of radio signals.

**MEDIA**

### BEAMING SIGNALS INTO SPACE

Radio telescope dishes can also be used to send signals into space. In the 1977 science-fiction film *Close Encounters of the Third Kind* the US military sent out signals in order to contact an Unidentified Flying Object (UFO) that landed on Earth, abducted people and then flew away.

# Terrestrial observatories

Observatories are special sites from which to view the night sky. People set up the first observatories thousands of years ago. Once the telescope was invented in the 1600s, new observatories were set up, first in Europe, then in America.

From the late 17th century, many nations competed to build bigger and better observatories. The observations made at those sites were used both to study the Universe and to measure time accurately.

## What is an observatory like?

Most terrestrial, or ground-based, observatories contain optical and infrared telescopes. So that the stars can be seen clearly, these observatories are sited in parts of the world where the air is as clear and cloudless as possible, and which are far from city lights. They are usually built on high mountains, because the air is thinner and cleaner there. The telescopes and other delicate equipment are protected from the weather by moveable domes, with slits in them through which the telescope can observe the sky.

**OBSERVATORY SITES**

Mount Graham International Observatory, Arizona, USA: includes the Large Binocular Telescope, one of the world's most powerful optical telescopes.

Laser Interferometer Gravitational-Wave Observatory, Louisiana, USA: the most sensitive experimental gravitational-wave observatory.

Super-Kamiokande, Mount Kamioka, Japan: one of the most successful neutrino observatories.

**Below: Several observatories share the heights of Mauna Kea in Hawaii, including the Keck.**

Secondary mirror

Primary mirror

## Keck Observatory

The Keck Observatory was built on an extinct volcano in Hawaii. Its twin telescopes have mirrors 10m across. Each mirror is made of 36 smaller mirrors, all of which can move separately. Using a technique called interferometry, the two telescopes can work together to make better observations than each could alone.

## Detecting gravitational waves

When objects move, they make tiny wobbles in the time and space around them, which spread out like ripples. These ripples are called gravitational waves. So far it has proved impossible to measure them. The European Gravitational Observatory near Pisa, Italy, uses mirrors and light beams in long tubes to try to detect these waves from fast-moving black holes, and from the Big Bang (see p.94).

## Neutrino telescopes

Neutrinos are tiny particles that hurtle through space in huge numbers. Because they pass through almost anything, they are nearly impossible to detect. Several neutrino telescopes have been built down old mines, where no other form of radiation can penetrate. Each includes vast amounts of liquid. Occasionally a neutrino changes the liquid slightly, and this change triggers sensitive detectors.

# SPACE OBSERVATORIES

PUTTING AN OBSERVATORY IN ORBIT IS A MAJOR FEAT, BUT IT IS THE ONLY WAY TO MAKE OBSERVATIONS OF SOME TYPES OF RADIATION. THIS IS BECAUSE THE EARTH'S ATMOSPHERE BLOCKS THEM OUT BEFORE THEY CAN REACH THE GROUND.

Aurora

Meteors

Weather balloon

Passenger plane

A view through the atmosphere

## WHERE SPACE STARTS

Space is often defined as starting at 100km above Earth, but there is no sudden beginning to space: as one rises higher and higher from the Earth, the air gets gradually thinner. The thinner the air, the more radiation is available to observe, so balloons, planes and the space shuttle have all been used as temporary observatories. However, it is necessary to reach a height of about 300km to put a space observatory satellite in orbit. Only there is the air thin enough not to slow down the observatory and cause it to crash back to Earth.

**The space shuttle *Ende***
**approaches the Hubble S**
**Telescope to repair it.**

## ATMOSPHERIC EFFECTS

The atmosphere causes many problems for ground-based telescopes. For one thing, it is often full of clouds that make most observations impossible. Even when there are no clouds, the air is in constant motion, which limits the types of observation that can be made. This motion is why stars twinkle: in space they shine steadily. And, there are many types of radiation that the air itself blocks, including most infrared and ultraviolet and practically all X-rays and gamma rays.

## HUBBLE VISION

The Hubble Space Telescope has provided us with some of the best views of planets, galaxies and other objects in space. But it was nearly a complete failure – a tiny error in the construction of its main mirror led to blurry images. So, in 1993 a space shuttle was sent to repair it. It was one of the most challenging shuttle missions, but it was a success.

# Great astronomers

There are two kinds of astronomers – observational astronomers watch and measure the stars, and theoretical astronomers develop mathematical theories to explain how the Universe and its contents work.

### Galileo Galilei (1564–1642)
Galileo was an Italian scientist who, in 1609, was the first person to use a telescope to study the night sky. Within a few hours, he had found out what the surface of our Moon looks like. He also discovered four moons in orbit around the planet Jupiter. In 1610, he was the first to see that the Milky Way is made of stars. Galileo was also an important theoretical astronomer, explaining sunspots and comets, and trying to prove that the Earth orbits the Sun. Though not all his conclusions were correct, it was he who really started the modern science of astronomy.

### Sir Isaac Newton (1643–1727)
Newton invented the reflecting telescope, which became the most useful astronomical instrument for centuries. His theories explained the motions of the Moon, planets and comets properly for the first time. Newton proved that the Moon orbits the Earth due to the force of gravity. He worked out the mathematics that describes how gravity changes depending on the masses and distances of the objects involved. He also showed how to use his laws of gravity and of motion to work out the movements of planets and comets.

### Edwin Hubble (1889–1953)
Hubble, along with his colleagues, made two of the greatest scientific discoveries of the 20th century. The first was that the enormous group of stars (called the Milky Way Galaxy), of which our Sun is a member, is one of many similar systems. This showed that the Universe was far larger than had previously been believed. The second discovery was that the whole Universe is expanding. This suggested that the Universe had come into existence long ago and had been expanding from then on, rather than having always existed.

Galileo – observer and theoretician

Newton – theoretician

Hubble – observer and theoretician

WEBSITES ON SPACE AND TIME

*http://apod.nasa.gov/apod/astropix.html*   A new astronomy picture every day.

*http://eclipse.gsfc.nasa.gov/eclipse.html*   Past and future eclipses.

*http://skyview.gsfc.nasa.gov*   A virtual observatory.

*www.popastro.com/youngstargazers/skyguide/index.php*   Looks at what is visible in the sky tonight.

*www.windows2Universe.org/mythology/stars.html*   Myths and legends of the stars.

# THE SOLAR SYSTEM

The Earth, Sun and Moon are all members of the Solar System, along with seven other planets, many moons, comets, asteroids and meteorites. The planets occupy only a small area in the middle of the Solar System. Around them is a huge disc and then a vast cloud containing billions of pieces of rock, metal and ice.

# The Sun and its planets

The Sun is at the centre of the Solar System. It is more massive than all the planets put together. Everything in the Solar System is spinning, and everything goes around the Sun or some other astronomical object.

There are two kinds of planet in the Solar System. The inner four are the rocky, or terrestrial (Earth-like), planets: Mercury, Venus, Earth and Mars. They are made of rocks and metals. The outer four planets are Jupiter, Saturn, Uranus and Neptune. They are gas giants, with rings, deep cloudy atmospheres and many moons.

## Discovering the Solar System

Just five planets, along with the Sun and the Moon, can be seen in the sky without a telescope. So, until the first telescopes were made in the 17th century, the rest of the Solar System was invisible and unknown. Since then, two more planets and many moons and comets have been discovered. A number of them have been visited by spacecraft from Earth.

## Gravity

Gravity is the force that holds you to the ground and keeps the planets going around the Sun. Each object pulls on every other with the force of gravity. But only large objects like moons and planets are massive enough for their gravity to be noticeable.

**PLANET KEY**

1. Mercury
2. Venus
3. Earth
4. Mars
5. Jupiter
6. Saturn
7. Uranus
8. Neptune

## Orbits and years

The Sun's gravity pulls harder on planets close to it, so those planets have to orbit (go around) it quickly to avoid being pulled in. The time taken for a planet to orbit the Sun once is its year. So, because inner planets travel fast, and also because their orbits are small, their years are short.

6

7

8

# HOW THE SYSTEM FORMED

THE SOLAR SYSTEM BEGAN TO FORM ABOUT 4.5 BILLION YEARS AGO, INSIDE A HUGE, DARK SPACE-CLOUD. THE CLOUD WAS DISTURBED BY A SUPERNOVA (SEE P.75) AND PARTS OF IT COLLAPSED. ONE OF THESE AREAS EVENTUALLY FORMED THE SUN AND PLANETS.

## CLOUD COLLAPSE

Once a part of the cloud started to collapse, the gravity-pull of its particles drew it tightly together. As it shrank, it began to spin and formed a disc in space. In the middle of the disc, the cloud material became closely packed, forming a proto-Sun.

## THE YOUNG SUN

The particles in the core of the disc were so tightly packed together that they kept crashing into each other, and this made them get hotter and hotter. Eventually, they were so hot that the core of the disc started to glow with light and heat. The core was now a baby version of our Sun, called a T Tauri star.

## NEW WORLDS

The T Tauri star kept getting hotter until nuclear reactions began in its core (see pp.68–69). It was now a true star. Meanwhile, material in the rest of the spinning disc gathered together due to the pull of gravity. The material formed rings, which later turned into many planets – perhaps as many as 30.

## DESTRUCTION

Many of the new-born planets crashed into one other. Sometimes, they stuck together to form new, larger planets. In other cases they destroyed one another. Eventually, only the eight planets we know today remained. Some of them captured wandering small worlds, which went into orbit around them as moons.

# Mercury

Mercury is the smallest planet and the closest to the Sun. Because Mercury has a thin atmosphere, heat escapes from it quickly. After the Sun sets on Mercury, its nights are cold.

The Sun is so close to Mercury that it shines very brightly there: more than six times as brightly as on Earth. The very thin atmosphere means that the sky is black.

**Left:** Mercury is covered in craters caused by impacts from space objects.

*Mariner 10*

**Solar panel, to turn sunlight into electricity**

**MERCURY FACTS**

**Discoverer**
Unknown
**Discovery date**
Prehistoric
**Average distance from Sun**
58 million km
**Year length**
87.97 Earth days
**Rotation period**
58.65 Earth days
**Equatorial radius**
2,440km
(38% of Earth)
**First reached**
1974, by *Mariner 10*
**Gravity compared to Earth**
38%
**Main atmospheric gases**
Oxygen (42%)
Sodium (29%)
Hydrogen (22%)
Helium (6%)
Potassium (1%)
**Number of moons**
0

## Mercury overview

Mercury spins very slowly, which means that it has very long days and nights. It also has a very short year – it does not even last for two Mercurian days. It is so hot on Mercury that some metals, such as tin and lead, would melt there. Like Earth, Mercury has an internal magnetic field that acts like an enormous bar magnet with a North and South Pole. One of the questions the *Messenger* probe is set to answer is why the magnetic properties of the inner planets vary with time.

## Missions to Mercury

Only two spacecraft have travelled to Mercury. *Mariner 10* flew past the planet three times in 1974 and 1975. It took photos of about half the surface. The second probe, *Messenger,* was launched in August 2004 and is still very active. Its name reflects the type of astronomy it will carry out – *ME*rcury *S*urface, *S*pace *EN*vironment, *GE*ochemistry and *R*anging. It has already completed hundreds of orbits of Mercury and sent back many photographs and measurements.

**Arm with devices to measure magnetic fields**

**Right: *Messenger* probe above the surface of Mercury.**

## Weird world

*Mariner 10* discovered a huge crater on Mercury that was then named Caloris Basin. It was formed billions of years ago when an enormous object struck Mercury. The impact was so powerful that shock waves travelled through the whole planet. At the opposite side of Mercury to the basin is a strange jumbled landscape, where the shock waves met up again.

MYTHOLOGY

**PLANET GOD**

All of the planets are named after Roman and Greek gods. Mercury was supposed to be a fast-moving Roman god with wings on his shoes and on his hat, too – a great name for the fastest planet. He was also the messenger of the other gods and delivered dreams to people as they slept.

# Venus

Venus is the planet that comes closest to Earth and, because it is also close to the Sun and covered in bright clouds, it often shines brightly in our sky.

The surface of Venus is dark and very hot. Drops of acid fall from the clouds, and lightning often flashes in the orange-yellow sky.

## Venus overview

On Venus, the days last longer than the years. On the surface, the Sun is never seen. The temperature is almost the same all day and night, all year and all over the planet.

**VENUS FACTS**
**Discoverer**
Unknown
**Discovery date**
Prehistoric
**Average distance from Sun**
108 million km
**Year length**
224.70 Earth days
**Rotation period**
243.02 Earth days
**Equatorial radius**
6,052km
(95% of Earth)
**First reached**
1962, by *Mariner 2*
**Gravity compared to Earth**
90%
**Main atmospheric gases**
Carbon dioxide (96%)
Nitrogen (4%)
**Number of moons**
0

Maat Mons is shown in this computer-generated three-dimensional perspective of the surface of Venus.

Below: *Magellan* made radar maps of Venus.

Radar aerials

## Missions to Venus

Many spacecraft have visited Venus, but landers are quickly destroyed by the dangerous atmosphere there. However, some have sent photos and information back to Earth first.

## Volcanoes on Venus

Venus has hundreds of volcanoes, but no one is sure if any still erupt. Some volcanoes are called Arachnoids because they are surrounded by patterns of ridges that make them look like spiders.

**About 80% of sunlight is reflected.**

**Each of the three cloud layers contains a different size of sulphuric acid droplets.**

**Infra-red is caught by carbon dioxide in the atmosphere, making it hotter.**

**Surface is heated by sunlight, making it glow with infrared radiation.**

**Only 20% of sunlight reaches the surface.**

## Atmosphere

Although it is not the closest planet to the Sun, Venus is the hottest one. This is because of its atmosphere, which contains gases that trap the Sun's heat. This is known as the greenhouse effect.

HISTORY

**TRANSITS OF VENUS**

When Venus passes directly between the Earth and the Sun, it can be seen as a black dot on the Sun's face. This is called a transit. Expeditions were once sent to distant parts of the world to observe transits, as this allowed the distance from the Earth to the Sun to be worked out.

# Earth

The Earth, our home in space, is the third planet from the Sun, and the only one with oceans on its surface. As far as we know, it is the only planet on which life exists.

For thousands of years, people thought that the Earth was the centre of the Universe. It was only in the 1500s that scientists proved that it is really a planet in constant orbit around the Sun.

Below: From the International Space Station, the Earth can be seen as a shining blue and white planet.

**EARTH FACTS**

**Average distance from Sun**
150 million km

**Year length**
365 or 366 days: average 365.26 days

**Rotation period**
23.93 hours

**Equatorial radius**
6,378km

**Mass**
5.97 trillion trillion kg

**Average density**
5,515kg per cubic metre

**Gravitational acceleration near surface**
9.81m per second per second

**Main atmospheric gases**
Nitrogen (78%)
Oxygen (21%)
Trace gases (1%)

**Number of moons**
1

## Earth overview

The Earth is the densest planet in the Solar System – that is, it has the most mass squeezed into its volume. It also has the largest moon in proportion to its own size, and a strong magnetic field. This magnetic field is essential to us, as it protects the Earth from the disruptive effects of the solar wind (see p.71). We are also protected by Earth's atmosphere, which stops most dangerous types of radiation from reaching the surface.

## Inside the Earth

The outer layer of the Earth, on which we live, is called the crust. It covers the whole planet and extends under the seas. Underneath it is a thick rocky layer called the mantle and beneath that is the core. The core is extremely hot and made mainly of the metals iron and nickel.

Crust

Mantle

Outer core (liquid)

Inner core (solid)

## Why is there life on Earth?

Living things were able to evolve on Earth for two main reasons: our planet has enough mass to hold on to a thick atmosphere, and it is the right temperature for water to be a liquid in some places.

# The Moon

The Moon is by far the closest astronomical object to us. It shines by reflecting sunlight onto the Earth. The part of the Moon lit by the Sun changes as the Moon moves, which is why it seems to change shape.

**MOON FACTS**
**Average distance from Earth**
384,000km
**Time to go around Earth**
27.32 days
**Rotation period**
27.32 days
**Equatorial radius**
1,738km
(27% of Earth)
**First reached**
1959, by lander *Luna 1*
**Gravity compared to Earth**
17%
**Main atmospheric gases**
None

Because the Moon is so small and light, its gravity-pull is very weak. This means that astronauts on the Moon weigh about one-sixth of the amount that they do on Earth.

## World without weather

The weak lunar gravity means that the Moon cannot hold on to an atmosphere. This lack of atmosphere means that there is no weather on the Moon. Because of this, the footprints left by astronauts in the 1960s are still there.

## Moonbirth

The Moon is 4.5 billion years old – nearly as old as the Earth. It was formed as the result of a small planet crashing into Earth. The planet was destroyed. Rubble from it and the Earth was thrown into orbit and the Moon formed from this rubble. Since then the Moon has slowly moved away from Earth. It is now retreating at the same speed as fingernails grow.

**Left: *Surveyor 3* landed on the Moon in 1967.**

## The hidden face

As the Moon goes around the Earth, it turns at exactly the same rate. This means that it always shows us the same side. The far side can only be seen by spacecraft. It looks quite different from the near side as it has no large 'seas'.

## Moonscape

From Earth we can see great dark patches on the Moon. These are called seas but are really plains of cold, hard lava. Brighter patches are mountainous areas. The Moon is covered in bowl-shaped depressions called craters. These are caused by huge objects crashing into its surface.

## Tides

As the Moon goes around the Earth, it pulls on our oceans with the force of gravity. Together with the Sun's gravity, this causes the tides. When the Sun and Moon pull in the same direction, tides are at their highest.

# Mars

In some ways, Mars is quite like Earth. Its day is nearly the same length, its temperature is not much lower and some of its weather is similar, too.

The temperature on the surface of Mars changes throughout the year, partly because it has seasons (see p.15) but also because it has an oval orbit which means that its distance from the Sun varies greatly.

Deimos

Phobos

*Phobos* and *Deimos* are Greek words meaning 'fear' and 'terror'.

**MARS FACTS**
**Discoverer**
Unknown
**Discovery date**
Prehistoric
**Average distance from Sun**
228 million km
**Year length**
1.88 Earth years
**Rotation period**
24.6 hours
**Equatorial radius**
3,396km
(53% of Earth)
**First reached**
1965, by *Mariner 4*
**Gravity compared to Earth**
38%
**Main atmospheric gases**
Carbon dioxide (95%)
Nitrogen (3%)
Argon (2%)
**Number of moons**
2

## Mars overview

Mars is the fourth and final rocky planet from the Sun. It is covered in deserts, with huge canyons far larger than those on Earth. The soil is reddish because the iron in it has turned to rust. Its atmosphere is very thin. When the planet is coldest, about one-third of the atmosphere freezes solid.

## Mars moons

Mars has two tiny moons – Phobos and Deimos – that are two of the darkest objects in the Solar System. They are probably asteroids (see p.58) that have been trapped by the gravity of Mars. Both moons always keep the same face turned towards Mars.

## Exploring Mars

Mars is the best-known of the planets because its surface can be seen by Earth-based telescopes and it has been explored by more spacecraft than any other planet. The above picture was taken by the *Pathfinder* lander and shows the *Sojourner* rover beside a big boulder.

## Volcanoes on Mars

There are several volcanoes on Mars, including the largest in the Solar System, Olympus Mons. It is three times the height of Mount Everest and covers an area the size of Ireland. It is thought to have last erupted about 25 million years ago.

*Mariner 9* orbited Mars in 1971.

MEDIA

**A BATTLE BETWEEN EARTH AND MARS**

In 1898 HG Wells wrote *The War of the Worlds*, a story about an invasion of Earth from Mars. In it, Martians conquer Earth but are then destroyed by germs in our atmosphere. When a radio version of this story was broadcast in the USA in 1938, some people thought it was a real report and panicked.

# LIFE ON MARS

EVER SINCE ASTRONOMERS THOUGHT THEY SAW CANALS ON MARS IN THE LATE 19TH CENTURY, PEOPLE HAVE SEARCHED FOR LIFE THERE. FIRST THEY USED TELESCOPES, THEN SPACECRAFT, LANDERS AND ROVERS.

**Water must have flowed over the surface of Mars for a long time.**

## WATER ON MARS

The canals of Mars were not real, but there are river beds there through which water once flowed, long ago when the atmosphere of Mars was thicker than it is now. The presence of water makes it more likely that life once existed on Mars. This area of the planet (right) was carved out by water about a million years ago. It was taken by the Mars *Reconnaissance* orbiter.

Ice cap

Ice cap

## MARTIAN ICE

In 2008, a pool of ice was found in a crater near the north pole of Mars. The high crater walls mean that the Sun never shines on it so the ice remains frozen.

**Left: The polar ice caps of Mars get bigger in the Martian winter and smaller in the summer.**

## LANDERS AND ROVERS

Three landers and three rovers have landed successfully on Mars. The first two were the *Viking* landers (one shown right), which discovered strange chemical activity in the soil in 1977. The *Sojourner* rover studied the Martian soil and atmosphere in 1997. The two latest rovers, *Spirit* (below) and *Opportunity*, arrived in 2004. They proved that liquid water once flowed on Mars. In 2008, the *Phoenix* lander found ice on Mars.

**Spirit has a robotic arm and four cameras. It gets its power from sunlight.**

# Jupiter

By far the largest and most massive planet, Jupiter is the fifth from the Sun and the first of the four gas giants. Like the rest, it has a deep, cold atmosphere, rings and many moons.

Four of Jupiter's moons are much larger than the rest and can be seen easily from Earth with a small telescope. They were discovered by Galileo in 1609 and are called the Galilean moons in his honour.

## JUPITER FACTS

**Discoverer**
Unknown
**Discovery date**
Prehistoric
**Average distance from Sun**
779 million km
**Year length**
11.86 Earth years
**Rotation period**
9.93 hours
**Equatorial radius**
71,492km
(11.2 times Earth)
**First reached**
1973, by *Pioneer 10*
**Gravity compared to Earth**
253%
**Main atmospheric gases**
Hydrogen (90%)
Helium (10%)
**Number of moons**
63

## Jupiter overview

Jupiter has an incredibly powerful magnetic field, about 20,000 times stronger than Earth's, and a system of thin faint rings, made from dust drawn from its inner moons. This giant world has no solid surface: below its atmosphere lies a thick layer of liquid hydrogen and helium, and under that is a layer of hydrogen that behaves like a liquid metal.

## The Great Red Spot

The Great Red Spot is a vast hurricane, large enough to swallow three planets the size of Earth, and it has existed for at least 300 years. Since the 1970s, its colour has changed from orange to dark brown.

Jupiter's surface and interior.

Liquid metallic hydrogen

Liquid hydrogen

Great Red Spot

Solid iron core

## Probes to Jupiter

Eight probes have explored
Jupiter. In the 1970s, the
*Pioneer* missions sent back the
first close-ups of the planet,
and the two *Voyagers* sent
back much more data and
discovered the rings. *Galileo*
(left) orbited Jupiter in 1995,
and in 2007 *New Horizons*
studied its moons.

## Galilean moons

## Europa and Ganymede

The icy surface of Europa is marked by
enormous cracks, and beneath it there is a
liquid ocean. Ganymede is made of rock and
ice, and is the largest moon in the Solar System.
It is bigger than the planet Mercury.

## Io and Callisto

The gravity-pulls of Jupiter and Europa produce
great heat inside Io, causing volcanoes to erupt
there constantly. Callisto, on the other hand, has
no volcanoes, but is covered in craters formed
by the impacts of meteoroids (see p.60).

# Saturn

Saturn is a cold, butterscotch-coloured world, ten times farther from the Sun than the Earth is. It is the least dense of all the planets, and less dense than water. That means that, if there was an ocean big enough, Saturn would float in it.

Saturn spins on its axis faster than any other planet. This makes its Equator bulge outwards and flattens it at the poles, so it is more grapefruit- than ball-shaped.

**SATURN FACTS**
**Discoverer**
Unknown
**Discovery date**
Prehistoric
**Average distance
from Sun**
1,433 million km
**Year length**
29.46 Earth years
**Rotation period**
10.57 hours
**Equatorial radius**
60,270km
(9.45 times Earth)
**First reached**
1979, by *Pioneer 11*
**Gravity compared
to Earth**
106%
**Main atmospheric
gases**
Hydrogen (96%)
Helium (3%)
Trace gases (1%)
**Number of moons**
At least 62

## Saturn overview

On Saturn, winds blow ten times faster than a hurricane on Earth. The outer part of the atmosphere is very hazy, which means that the cloud patterns beneath cannot be seen as clearly as those on Jupiter. About every 30 years, huge storms appear. They can be seen as white spots.

Artist's impression of Titan, with pools containing methane. On Earth, methane is used for fuel.

## Probes to Saturn

Saturn was visited by *Pioneer 11* in 1979 and *Voyagers 1* and *2* in 1980 and 1981. The *Cassini–Huygens* space probe went into orbit around Saturn in 2004 and sent the *Huygens* lander to the surface of Titan.

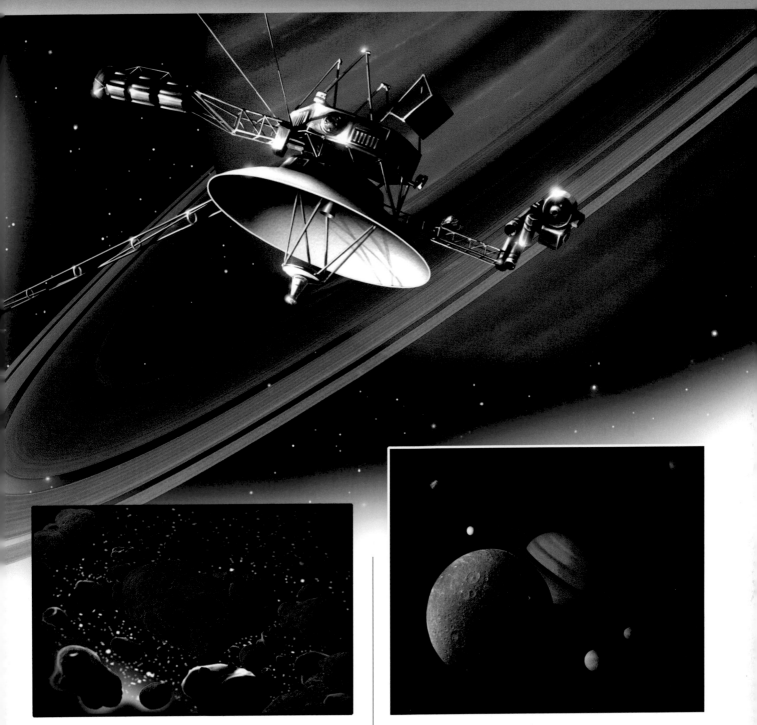

## Saturn's rings

Saturn's seven rings are the most massive and widest in the Solar System. They are made of lumps of dirty ice, from tiny fragments to pieces many metres across. The rings are hundreds of thousands of kilometres across, yet only a few metres thick in some places. They may be the remains of a moon destroyed long ago.

## Saturn's moons

Most of Saturn's moons were discovered by space probes. It is thought that the outer ones were captured by Saturn's gravity. The gravity-pulls of some of the moons make gaps in Saturn's ring-system. Saturn's largest moon, Titan, is the only moon in the Solar System with a thick atmosphere.

# Uranus

Uranus looks like a pale blue ball, with few cloud patterns visible on its surface. Under its thick atmosphere is a layer of frozen gases, and at the centre is a rocky core.

The other planets have magnetic fields with north and south poles that are close to the points (called rotational poles) about which the planets spin. Uranus is very different – its magnetic poles are a long way from its rotational poles.

## Uranus overview

Uranus is about twice as far from the Sun as Saturn and 19 times as far as Earth, so it receives little of the Sun's light and heat. This means it is a very cold place. All the gas giants make some heat of their own, but Uranus makes much less than the others. This means that it does not have the dramatic weather that the other giant planets do.

## Probes to Uranus

Only one probe has visited Uranus: *Voyager 2*, in 1986. The spacecraft took nine years to reach Uranus, and passed within 82,000km of the planet. It studied the atmosphere of Uranus, its largest moons, strange magnetic field and rings before continuing its journey to Neptune.

**URANUS FACTS**
**Discoverer**
William Herschel
**Discovery date**
13 March 1781
**Average distance from Sun**
2,877 million km
**Year length**
84.32 Earth years
**Rotation period**
17.24 hours
**Equatorial radius**
25,560km
(4 times Earth)
**First reached**
1986, by *Voyager 2*
**Gravity compared to Earth**
89%
**Main atmospheric gases**
Hydrogen (about 83%)
Helium (about 15%)
Methane (about 2%)
**Number of moons**
27

## The moons of Uranus

Ten of Uranus's moons were discovered by *Voyager 2*, and all of them are named after characters in the plays of William Shakespeare or the poems of Alexander Pope. Miranda, the fifth-largest moon, has a strange jumbled surface – it is possible that it may have shattered millions of years ago and been pulled together again by gravity.

## The rings of Uranus

Nine of Uranus's rings were discovered in 1977 when they caused light from a star behind them to flicker as they passed in front of it. Two more rings were found by *Voyager 2* and the rest by the Hubble Space Telescope.

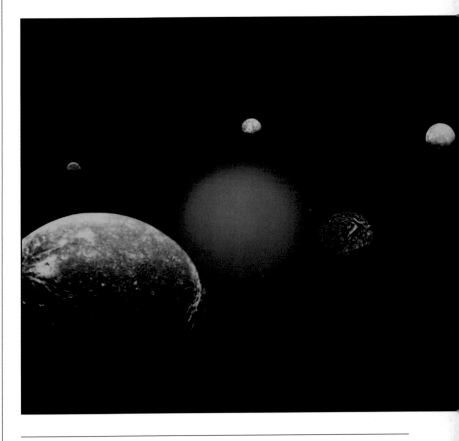

## Sideways spin

As Uranus goes around the Sun, its axis points almost directly at the Sun. When it does, days and nights there can sometimes each last for more than 40 years.

**ASTRONOMER**

**DISCOVERY OF URANUS**

Uranus can just be seen without a telescope, but it was not identified until 1781, when William Herschel spotted it through his home-made telescope. Herschel wanted to name the object Georgium Sidus (George's Star), in honour of Great Britain's King George III, but astronomers from other countries objected and it was named after a Greek god of the sky, Ouranos. Uranus was the first planet to be discovered since ancient times.

# Neptune

Neptune is the most distant planet from the Sun. This means it has the longest year of all. From Neptune, the Sun looks like a bright star, and the planet receives little heat from it.

Neptune has a deep, very cold atmosphere. It is so similar to that of Uranus that it is puzzling that the two planets are different colours. Underneath there is a thick, icy layer with a small rocky core in the centre.

**NEPTUNE FACTS**
**Discoverer**
Johann Gottfried Galle
**Discovery date**
23 September 1846
**Average distance from Sun**
4,503 million km
**Year length**
164.79 Earth years
**Rotation period**
16.11 hours
**Equatorial radius**
24,760km
(3.88 times Earth)
**First reached**
1989, by *Voyager 2*
**Gravity compared to Earth**
114%
**Main atmospheric gases**
Hydrogen (80%)
Helium (19%)
Methane (1%)
**Number of moons**
13

## Exploring Neptune

Only one probe has visited Neptune: *Voyager 2*. It reached Neptune in 1989, after a 12-year journey. *Voyager 2* discovered that Neptune is a world of storms, and saw strange jets of gas and dust on Neptune's moon Triton. It also studied Neptune's rings and discovered six new moons. Because Neptune is so far away, the radio signals from *Voyager* took four hours to reach Earth.

## Neptune's weather

Neptune makes its own heat and this drives a stormy weather system. It has the highest winds in the Solar System, enormous black storm-spots and white, fast-moving clouds.

## Neptune's moons

Neptune has one large moon, Triton (right), and 12 smaller ones. Triton has jets of nitrogen gas and dust that soar high above the surface before being knocked sideways by high-speed winds. Triton was discovered only 17 days after Neptune itself. It was probably not formed near Neptune but was captured by its gravity. The image on the left is an imaginary view from Neptune's tiny moon Proteus, showing the shadow of Triton on Neptune's cloudy face.

## Neptune's rings

Neptune's rings are made of dusty ice particles. They were discovered from Earth in 1984 but were only properly studied by *Voyager 2*, which found that there are five of them. The rings are much thinner in some places than others, so that from Earth they look like arcs rather than rings. This may be caused by the gravity of some of Neptune's moons.

**ASTRONOMER**

**DISCOVERY OF NEPTUNE**
After Uranus had been studied for some years, it was noticed that it was not moving as expected. Perhaps another planet was pulling it off course? The position of the planet was worked out mathematically and astronomers searched the sky in that area. In 1846 Johann Gottfried Galle, a German astronomer, spotted a new planet from the Berlin Observatory (above). It was called Neptune after the Roman god of the sea.

# TINY WORLDS

As well as large objects such as
the Sun, its planets and their moons,
there are countless smaller worlds
that are also members of
our Solar System.

Sun

Mercury

Venus

Earth

Mars

Ceres

Jupiter

Asteroid Belt

Satu

## ASTEROIDS

There are billions of lumps of rock or metal called
asteroids. Most can be found in the Asteroid Belt,
between Mars and Jupiter. On the right is asteroid Ida,
with a tiny asteroid called Dactyl in orbit around it.

## DWARF PLANETS

Dwarf planets are large enough for their gravity to give them rounded shapes. Only five are known but there are probably many more that are too small and dim to have been discovered yet. This dwarf planet, Ceres, is the closest to us and the smallest. Haumea, Makemake and Eris have all been discovered since 2004.

Neptune

Huamea

Eris

Makemake

Kuiper Belt

Pluto

Oort Cloud

## KUIPER BELT

The Kuiper Belt, a detail of which is shown below, is a ring of comet-like objects. Although 70,000 are more than 100km across, most are too small to see from Earth. The outer part of the belt is known as the Scattered Disc.

## PLUTO

Until 2006, dwarf planet Pluto was classified as a planet. Made of rock and ice, it has three moons. Pluto's oval orbit means its distance from the Sun changes greatly. It has an atmosphere when it is close to the Sun, but the gases freeze as it moves away.

# Space rubble

The Solar System is full of dust, grit and rubble, mostly left over from its formation. Some of this material can be seen as a faint glow of light in the sky just before sunrise or after sunset. This is called the zodiacal light.

Tiny pieces of space-dust called micrometeorites constantly drift down to Earth, while larger pieces of falling material can be seen as meteors (shooting stars) as they burn up in the atmosphere.

## Uses of meteorites

Before people knew how to get metals from rocks, some meteorites were an important source of iron. A large iron meteorite that fell in Greenland about 10,000 years ago was used by the local people for centuries to make tools from. Nowadays, meteorites are useful samples of the material from which the planets formed.

### METEORITES

Objects that fall to the Earth's surface from space are called meteorites. (They are called meteoroids while they are still in space.) Most meteorites are made of stone, but some are made from iron, or a mixture of stone and iron. The largest known meteorite, called Hoba West, weighs about 60 tonnes.

Meteorites

## Impact craters

Large meteorites can leave craters on the Earth. Mercury, the Moon and several of the moons of other planets are covered in craters caused by meteoroids or asteroids (see p.58). This crater is in Arizona, USA, and was caused by an impact about 50,000 years ago.

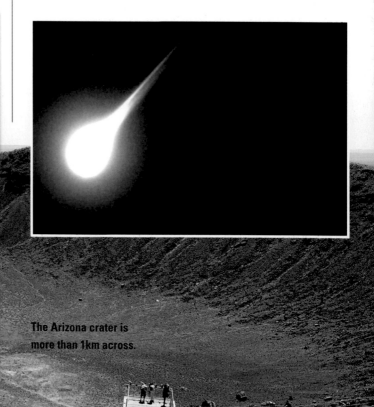

The Arizona crater is more than 1km across.

## Down to Earth

As a meteoroid falls through the atmosphere, it squashes the air in front of it, generating so much heat that the meteoroid begins to glow and quickly turns to hot gas and dust. The largest meteors are called fireballs. Sometimes, a fireball can break up on its way through the atmosphere. Some large meteoroids reach the ground before they are destroyed. What is left is called a meteorite.

Fireball

Fireball breaking up          Meteors

Meteorite impact

**Below: Leonid meteor shower at Monteromano, Italy.**

## Meteor showers

Some meteoroids are parts of asteroids, while others come from trails of dust and grit left behind by comets. When Earth passes through one of these trails, a whole 'shower' of meteors appears. The Leonid shower appears around 17 November. It gets its name from Leo, the constellation in which the meteors appear.

# Comets and the Oort Cloud

Comets are visitors from the edge of the Solar System.
They appear as misty streaks that glow in the night sky.
Comets often last for many nights before fading away.

Comets are lumps of dirty ice that make
long journeys through space. As they
approach the Sun, some of the ice turns
to long trailing tails of gas and dust.

**Bluish tail of gas**

**The misty area
around the nucleus
is called the coma.**

**Whitish tail of dust**

**Tails are often over 100
million kilometres long.**

**Cometary nucleus is
made of ice and grit**

## Death from space

Sixty-five million years ago the
dinosaurs were wiped out. They had
been the most successful creatures
on Earth for the previous 160 million
years. It is thought that a comet
crashed into Earth, and so much dust
was thrown up that the sky was
darkened for months. Because
sunlight was cut off, the Earth cooled
and the dinosaurs could not survive.

## Jupiter impact

In 1994, comet Shoemaker-Levy 9 broke up and many
of its fragments crashed onto the planet Jupiter, leaving
disturbances in its atmosphere. Jupiter's strong gravity
means that it is hit much more often by comets than the
other planets are.

## Oort Cloud

Some comets come from an area called the Oort Cloud, which is the outermost part of the Solar System. Others come from the Scattered Disc, an area outside the Kuiper Belt (see p.59). Comets start to move towards the Sun from the cloud or disc when they are disturbed by the gravity of other objects. Oort Cloud comets are disturbed by passing stars, while it is the outer planets that affect the Scattered Disc.

## Comet probes

The *Stardust* probe was launched in 1999 and successfully collected dust from the comet Wild 2 in 2004. The probe returned the sample to Earth in 2006 and went on to visit comet Tempel 1 in 2011. Tempel 1 had been visited by another probe, *Deep Impact*, in 2005.

ASTRONOMER

**HALLEY'S COMET**

Edmond Halley (1656–1742) realized that some comets return regularly to Earth. He studied historical records and predicted that one comet, now named after him, would return in 1758. Sure enough, it did. Since then, records of every visit of Halley's comet have been found, going back to 240BCE.

# Discovery timeline

Until the telescope was invented in 1609, the planets were just dots in the sky, but since then a vast number of discoveries have been made about them and the rest of the Solar System.

**OBSERVING THE PLANETS**

- **1610** Galileo Galilei observes four of Jupiter's moons, the first moons of any other planet's to be discovered.
- **1655** Saturn's rings are discovered, by Christiaan Huygens.
- **1705** Edmond Halley shows that comets can return many times.
- **1781** Uranus is discovered by William Herschel.
- **1846** Neptune is observed by Johann Gottfried Galle.
- **1930** Pluto, then classed as a planet, is discovered by Clyde Tombaugh.
- **1959** First probe to fly past the Moon, *Luna 1*.

- **1959** Far side of the Moon is seen for the first time, by *Luna 3*.
- **1962** First probe to successfully fly by another planet: *Mariner 2*.
- **1965** First probe to reach Mars: *Mariner 4*.
- **1969** First humans land on the Moon: two US astronauts in a lunar module.
- **1970** First rover to explore the Moon: *Lunokhod 1*.
- **1973** First probe to reach Jupiter: *Pioneer 10*.
- **1974** First probe to reach Mercury: *Mariner 10*.
- **1979** First probe to reach Saturn: *Pioneer 11*.

- **1986** First probe to reach Uranus: *Voyager 2*.
- **1986** First probes to reach a comet – Halley's comet: *Vega 1, Vega 2, Giotto, Suisei* and *Sakigake*.
- **1989** First probe to reach Neptune: *Voyager 2*.
- **1991** First probe to reach an asteroid – 951 Gaspra: *Galileo*.
- **2005** *Huygens* becomes the first probe to land on the moon of another planet, Saturn's moon Titan. *Deep Impact* becomes the first probe to make contact with a comet – Tempel 1.
- **2006** Pluto is reclassified as a dwarf planet.

**The Solar System: The Sun, eight planets and our moon**

WEBSITES ON THE SOLAR SYSTEM

*http://science.nationalgeographic.com/science/space/solar-system*  Explore the Solar System.

*http://starchild.gsfc.nasa.gov/docs/StarChild/solar_system_level1/solar_system.html*  Solar System facts.

*www.bbc.co.uk/science/space/solarsystem*  Science of the Solar System.

*www.jpl.nasa.gov/solar-system/index.cfm*  Solar System simulator.

*www.kidsastronomy.com/solar_system.htm*  Journey through the Solar System.

# STARS
# AND GALAXIES

Although the Universe is vast and contains trillions of
stars, we know a great deal about it. We understand how
stars are born and die, and why they are found in groups,
such as clusters and galaxies. But there are still many
mysteries to explore and questions to answer.

# What is a star?

The thousands of stars we can see on clear nights are enormous balls of glowing gas, far larger than the Earth.

By using a telescope, we can see millions of stars, but there are trillions more that are too far away for us to see at all.

## Star types

If a large number of stars are plotted on a graph based on their temperatures (decreasing from left to right across the graph) and their brightnesses (increasing from bottom to top), you get the pattern shown below. The positions of the stars form a diagonal – the main sequence – and a number of groups surrounding it. The main star types can be seen here. Supergiants are enormous and very bright. Giant stars are many times larger than the Sun, which is a main sequence star. White dwarfs are small and dim.

**STELLAR DISTANCES**
The distances to the stars can be measured by the time it takes their light to reach us. Light travels very fast, at 299,792km/s – it takes less than one-eighth of a second to go around the Earth.

The nearest star to us is the Sun, which is 8.1 light minutes away.

The next closest star is Proxima Centauri, 4.2 light years away. It is because the Sun is so much closer than the other stars that it looks so bright. Many of the stars we can see are actually much brighter than the Sun.

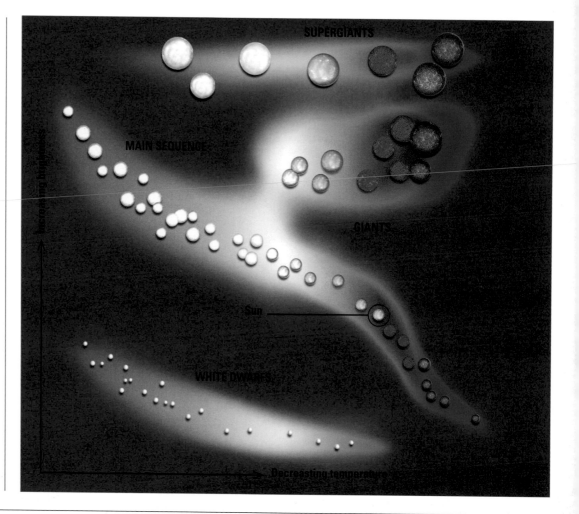

SUPERGIANTS

MAIN SEQUENCE

GIANTS

Sun

WHITE DWARFS

Decreasing temperature

Rigel – a
giant star

Sun – at the centre of
the main sequence

Sirius – a white dwarf

Aldebaran – a red giant, from the group
above the main sequence of stars

## The properties of stars

Stars have many different sizes, masses and
brightnesses. The biggest star, discovered in
2010, is about 320 times heavier than the Sun.
There are stars more than a million times
brighter than the Sun and one that is about
2,000 times wider.

## Temperatures and colours

The temperature of a star affects its colour.
Stars hotter than the Sun are bluish-white, while
cooler ones are yellow, orange, red or dark
brown. Stars are labelled with letters to show
how hot they are. The Sun is a G-type star.

O      B      A      F      G      K      M

# THE SUN

## THE GRAVITY OF THE SUN HOLDS THE SOLAR SYSTEM TOGETHER. TO AVOID BEING DRAGGED INTO THE SUN, THE EARTH AND OTHER PLANETS MUST KEEP GOING AROUND IT.

## TOO BRIGHT TO LOOK AT

The Sun is so bright that you must never look straight at it, because your eyes would be permanently damaged. Even wearing sunglasses is not sufficient protection from the Sun's rays. With a telescope you can project its image onto a flat sheet of paper and view it safely.

**The Sun's brightness means the Earth's surface is light during the day even when the sky is very cloudy.**

**SUN FACTS**

**Mass** 2 million trillion trillion tonnes (330,000 times Earth)

**Equatorial radius** 695,500km (109 times Earth)

**Temperature at centre** 15 million°C

**Temperature at visible surface** about 5,500°C

**Age** 4.6 billion years

**Gravity at visible surface** 28 times Earth

**Composition**
Hydrogen (74%)
Helium (25%)
Oxygen (1%)

**Below: The Sun is so bright that each centimetre of its surface gives out as much light as 250,000 candles.**

The Sun is not solid like the Earth. It is a ball of gas, made up of several different layers.

## SUNSHINE

The Sun shines because its enormous mass gives it very strong gravity. In its core, this gravity is so powerful that hydrogen atoms are crushed to form helium atoms. This is called a nuclear reaction. The reactions release energy that makes its way to the photosphere, where we see it as sunlight.

Convective zone: where swirling gases allow the Sun's energy to travel outwards.

Radiative zone: energy travels through this as streams of photons, which are like tiny lumps of energy.

Prominence: area where the convective zone becomes turbulent – creating huge surges of gas.

Core: where sunlight and other forms of energy are released.

Photosphere: the bright surface we can see. Outside it is the hot corona, too faint to see except during an eclipse.

## EXPLORING THE SUN

The first probes to study the Sun were the US spacecraft *Pioneers 5* to *9*, launched from 1959 onwards. Many others followed, including the 1980 Solar Maximum mission, sent when the Sun was especially active. The Solar Terrestrial Relations Observatory (STEREO) mission involves a pair of satellites making 3D maps of the Sun's activity.

# The Sun's surface

The outer layer of the Sun is full of activity, with constantly changing sunspots and other features. This activity increases and decreases over an 11-year period called the solar cycle.

The Sun's very strong magnetic field causes most of the effects astronomers can see on the Sun's surface.

Below: This red prominence is a huge surge of gas. Magnetism lifts it high above the Sun and holds it there for several days.

## Solar weather

To describe the activity on the Sun's surface, astronomers use the same terms as meteorologists do for the weather on Earth. They talk of winds and storms on the Sun. These movements or effects are not in the atmosphere, but rather they are on the surface or far out in space.

Above: A cluster of sunspots on the Sun's surface. They are seen to move because the Sun turns, but they shift across the surface, too.

Magnetic field joins the two sunspots together.

Sunspots form in pairs, each with an opposite magnetic pole.

Chromosphere

Solar wind particles are thrown off by the sunspots.

Photosphere

Sunspots

## Sunspots and faculae

Darker areas on the Sun are called sunspots. They are cooler than the surrounding areas, and are caused by strong magnetism. Their position varies and they may last for weeks or months. Bright areas are called faculae. The more sunspots there are, the more faculae there are, too.

## Granulation and flares

Granulation is the patchy appearance of the whole surface. Each granule is the top part of an area of convection or gas currents called a cell. Solar flares are huge explosions, while coronal mass ejections are vast bubbles of gas thrown off into space.

## The Sun and the Earth

A stream of electrically charged particles constantly flows away from the Sun in all directions in the same way that visible light waves stream out. It is called the solar wind and is strongest when the Sun is most active. We cannot see or feel the solar wind but it does affect the Earth by causing the northern and southern lights (also called auroras; see p.11) and by interfering with radio and television signals.

The shape of Earth's magnetic field is changed by the push of the solar wind.

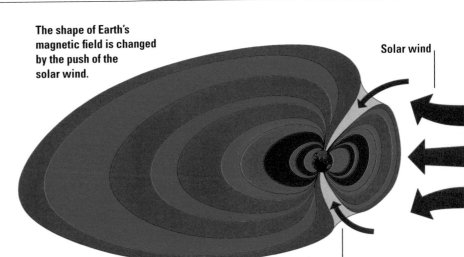

Solar wind

At the Earth's poles, solar wind particles move towards Earth along the magnetic field lines and cause auroras.

# Star birth

Stars are born, usually in groups, in dark molecular clouds of dust and gas. Star formation begins when passing stars or supernovae cause parts of these clouds to collapse.

At several places in the cloud, the material becomes very tightly packed and hot, and forms spinning discs. Stars form in the centres of these discs.

## Star stories

Because stars last much longer than people, we cannot watch them age. But we can find stars at all stages of their lives, and put them in order to understand how they develop. Our knowledge of physics helps us to explain this development, and computers are used to see whether these explanations are likely to be correct.

**Right: Stars form in the Pillars of Creation, part of the Eagle nebula.**

**Molecular cloud**

**Disc begins to form**

## Molecular clouds

Molecular clouds are enormous, often hundreds of light years across. The colder they are, the easier it is to make them collapse and start to form stars. The black areas in the picture are Bok globules, which are thick areas of dust and gas. Some have about the same mass as the Sun. Others are hundreds of times heavier. It is likely they will turn into spinning discs and then into stars.

## T Tauri stars

The spinning discs get very hot in their centres as matter there is squeezed by gravity. Eventually the centres start to glow and are called protostars. Our Sun may have once been a type of protostar called a T Tauri star. The orange star near the centre of this image was the first such star to be discovered. T Tauri stars are very active and appear to shine very brightly.

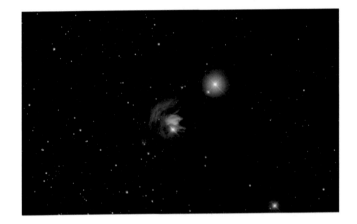

## Star populations

**Below: The diagram shows how the Sun was born. A star such as the Sun takes about 50 million years to form from an enormous collapsing molecular cloud.**

The Sun (right) and many other stars contain lots of different elements that were formed in older stars and later scattered through space. These older stars contained fewer different elements. The newer stars are called Population 2 stars, and the older ones are called Population 1 stars.

**Centre of disc glows, becoming a protostar**

**The protostar changes to a true star as nuclear reactions begin.**

**A young star burns brightly.**

# STAR DEATH

How long a star lives depends on its mass — the more massive, the shorter its life will be. The smallest stars last for several hundred billion years. Sun-like stars last for 10 billion years and very massive stars last for just a few million.

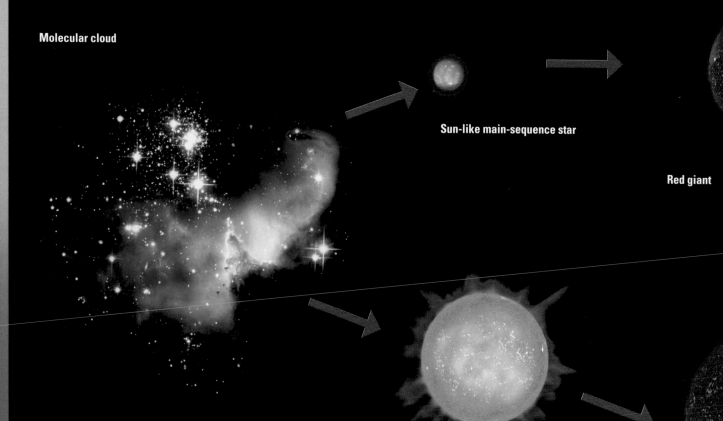

Molecular cloud

Sun-like main-sequence star

Red giant

Massive bright main-sequence star

Red supergiant

## MASSIVE STARS

When the core of a star more than nine times the mass of the Sun runs out of hydrogen, the star swells into a red supergiant and uses many other elements as fuel. When all of them run out, the star explodes as a supernova. It leaves behind a neutron star or, if the original star was more than 20 times the mass of the Sun, a black hole.

## SUN-LIKE STARS

When a Sun-like star runs out of hydrogen in its core, it begins to use helium instead, and swells to form a red giant. Once all the fuel is exhausted, the star's outer layers are thrown off to form a huge bubble of gas called a planetary nebula. The star's crushed core remains as a white dwarf, gradually cooling until it turns into a black dwarf.

## SUPERNOVAE

Supernova explosions are enormous, often brighter than all the other stars in a galaxy put together. Unlike the other stages in a star's life, which last for many millions of years, a supernova lasts for only a few days. The elements that were made by the star are scattered through space by the supernova. They form part of new stars and planets – and you, too. Another type of supernova is caused by the transfer of material from one star in a binary to the other (see pp.82–83).

**White dwarf**

**Pulsar (type of neutron star)**

**Planetary nebula**

**Supernova**

**Black hole**

# Neutron stars and pulsars

While a star is shining, the light and other energy streaming from it tries to make it swell. At the same time, its gravity tries to make it shrink. Usually the two forces are in balance so the star stays the same size.

**PULSARS**
Pulsars send out bursts of radio waves. The time between pulses is called a period.

**First pulsar to be discovered**
PSR B1919+21, in 1967

**First binary pulsar to be discovered**
PSR B1913+16, in 1974

**First pulsar with planets to be discovered**
PSR 1257+12, in 1992

**Fastest**
PSR J1748-2446ad, with a period of 0.001396 seconds

**Slowest**
J2144–3933, with a period of 8.51 seconds

**Closest to Earth**
PSR J0108-1431, 280 light years away

Most distant known

When the star runs out of fuel and stops shining, its gravity crushes it into a tiny object. Stars like the Sun shrink to white dwarfs, but larger ones shrink even further and become neutron stars.

## The Crab Nebula

In 1054CE, Chinese astronomers saw a new star that was so bright it could be seen in daylight. They called it a guest star, but we now know it was a supernova. The image shown right is what that area looks like now. It is called the Crab Nebula – a vast area of glowing gas that is getting larger all the time. Deep inside it is a pulsar.

## How pulsars work

Neutron stars have strong magnetic fields and they spin fast. These magnetic fields send narrow streams of radio waves across space. If these pass across Earth, they can be detected as beeps by radio telescopes. The neutron star is then called a pulsar. As they grow older and run out of energy, the beeps slow down. The Crab pulsar signal is slowing by about one hundred-thousandths of a second per year.

## Neutron stars

Neutron stars are only a few kilometres across, even though they weigh more than the Sun. They are covered in layers of iron. Their strong gravity means that their atmospheres are only a few centimetres thick. Neutron stars are the dead remains of stars from nine to 20 times the mass of the Sun. Stars that are even more massive form black holes (see p 79)

# BLACK HOLES

IF ENOUGH MATTER IS SQUEEZED INTO A SMALL ENOUGH SPACE, THE GRAVITY IS SO STRONG THAT NOTHING, NOT EVEN LIGHT, CAN ESCAPE. SO, THE OBJECT IS BLACK — A BLACK HOLE.

## HOW ARE BLACK HOLES SEEN?

Because they are black, only the effects of black holes can be seen. Each is surrounded by a disc of material that gradually falls in to it. This material releases energy as it does so, including powerful X-rays. The gravity of black holes can also bend the light from other stars. Both effects can be detected from Earth.

Below: A disc of gas and dust in the centre of a galaxy that probably has a supermassive black hole at its centre.

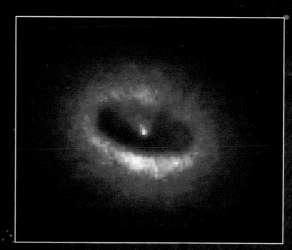

Some people think that black holes may one day allow spacecraft to travel great distances across the Universe – or even through time.

## DISCOVERING BLACK HOLES

The idea of a black hole was first suggested in 1783. In the early 20th century, Albert Einstein's work showed what they might be like, but no one really believed in them until a strong X-ray source called Cygnus X-1 was discovered. It is almost certainly a black hole.

If a spacecraft flew too close to a black hole, it would 'spaghettify' as the gravity tore it apart.

## SUPERMASSIVE BLACK HOLES

Not all black holes are the remains of dead stars. There are also supermassive black holes in the centres of galaxies. These may be more than one billion times the mass of the Sun. It is thought that they may grow from smaller black holes that draw in extra material, or they may form from collapsing gas clouds.

# Variable stars

Not all stars shine steadily. Some vary in brightness over hours, days, months or years. These stars are called variables. Those that change in a predictable way are called regular variables. Irregular variables are not predictable.

Stars can vary because they change size, or because a dust cloud or another star gets in the way of their light. On others, there are sudden enormous explosions.

**VARIABLE STARS**

**Eruptive**
Includes R Coronae Borealis stars, which produce sooty clouds, and flare stars.

**Pulsating**
Includes Miras, named after the first ever variable to be discovered (in 1596), and Cepheids.

**Rotating**
Pulsars, for example.

**Cataclysmic**
Includes novae and supernovae.

**Eclipsing**
Where binary stars pass across one another as seen from Earth.

## Star shells

The star at the centre of this image – V838 Monocerotis – is surrounded by dust shells. In 2002, a series of photos was taken of the star, which had released a great flare of light. As the light travelled from one dust shell to another, each lit up in turn (as shown in the four images on the right). No such outburst has been seen in any other star and its cause is uncertain, but it was extremely powerful, making the star about a million times brighter than the Sun. The star itself is enormous – more than 1,000 times as big as the Sun.

## Spotted stars

The Sun usually has many small spots on its surface. But some supergiant stars, like XX Trianguli (left), have spots so enormous that they cover a quarter of their surface or even more. This makes one side darker. Like all stars, XX Trianguli spins, so its brightness changes as seen from Earth. Like the Sun's spots, this one is probably caused by magnetic fields. It is about 1,000°C cooler than the rest of the star's surface.

## Cepheids

A Cepheid's period (the time it takes to vary) depends on how bright it is on average: brighter Cepheids have longer periods. This means that astronomers can work out the true brightness of a Cepheid by measuring its period. By comparing this with how bright it looks, its distance from Earth can be worked out.

**Monocerotis**

**20 May 2002**

**2 September 2002**

**28 October 2002**

**17 December 2002**

# BINARY STARS

Unlike our Sun, most of the stars in the sky exist in pairs. These stars are called binaries, or double stars. Usually they form close together, as part of the same cloud.

## A BINARY STAR SYSTEM

In a binary, the stars go around each other. If (as seen from Earth), they pass in front of each other, the binary changes in brightness and is called an eclipsing binary. If the stars are very close, they look like one star, but astronomers can measure the wobbles or colour changes caused by their motion. Binary stars are very useful because their masses can be worked out from such measurements.

## BINARY ORBITS

In a binary, how fast stars orbit one another depends on their masses and their distances apart. The stars in close binaries orbit in a few days, but the most widely separated ones take centuries to go around each other.

Common centre of gravity

Star 1

X

Star 2

## CONTACT BINARIES

In a contact binary, the stars are so close that the gravity of each pulls at the atmosphere of the other until the stars actually touch and mix. The stars often get in the way of each other as seen from Earth. This type of eclipsing binary is called a W Ursae Majoris variable.

Some binary stars may have planets going around them. The temperatures on the surfaces of the planets would change greatly as the planets move away from and towards each star, so it is unlikely that there are living things there.

# Star clusters

When lots of stars form from the same cloud, they often stay together for many millions of years as a star cluster. There are two types of cluster: globular clusters, which are roundish, and open clusters, which are scattered.

Globular clusters contain between several thousand and several million stars. From Earth, they look like misty balls of light. Open clusters contain dozens to thousands of stars.

### The Pleiades

The Pleiades open cluster (below) is easy to see from Earth because it is only about 440 light years away. It is also called the Seven Sisters because it contains seven bright stars (six in view here), as well as many dimmer ones. The Pleiades stars look fuzzy because they are passing through a dust cloud.

### CLUSTER NUMBERS

Clusters of stars are common. There are probably about 10,000 open clusters in the Milky Way. They are found in some other galaxies too, but only if stars are still forming there. There are probably fewer than 200 globular clusters in the Milky Way, but they are found in all large galaxies.

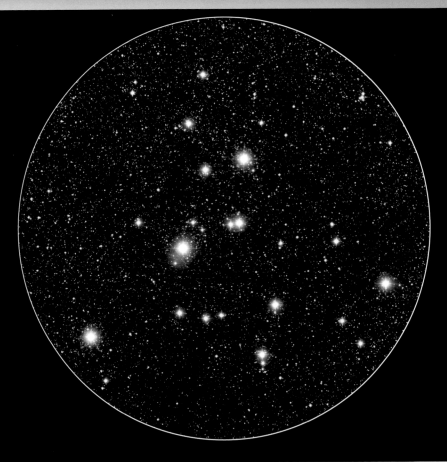

## Open cluster

Stars in open clusters drift away over periods of hundreds of millions of years. However, because they are still surrounded by the material they were made from, the stars that are lost are sometimes replaced by new ones. This cluster is called M39. The M stands for Messier, the name of the French astronomer Charles Messier, who discovered it in 1764. M39 is about 800 light years away from Earth, and is from 200 to 300 million years old. The stars in it are all about 300 million years old – much younger than the Sun. M39 is in the constellation of Cygnus, the Swan.

## Globular cluster

Globular clusters also drift apart, but their stronger gravity means that this process takes much longer than it does for open clusters, and they can last for billions of years. However, unlike open clusters, globulars never form new stars. This is M13. It is about 150 light years across and is about 25,000 light years from us. It contains several hundred thousand stars. On a very dark, clear night, M13 can just be seen with the naked eye. Because Messier's telescope was not of good enough optical quality to see details in it clearly, he described M13 as 'a nebula containing no stars'.

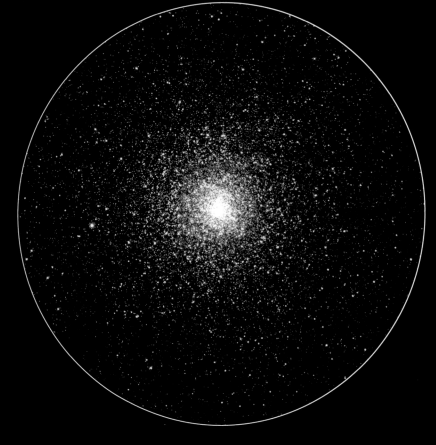

# SPACE CLOUDS

SPACE CONTAINS GAS ATOMS AND DUST PARTICLES. IN MOST PLACES THEY ARE FAR APART, BUT SOMETIMES THEY ARE GATHERED TOGETHER TO FORM CLOUD-LIKE OBJECTS CALLED NEBULAE.

## TYPES OF NEBULA

Where dust is thick and cold, it forms black clouds called dark nebulae, like the Horsehead Nebula, shown right. Where oxygen gas is heated by a nearby star, it glows red, forming an emission nebula. Dying stars make bubbles of gas called planetary nebulae, while supernovae leave behind nebulae called supernova remnants.

## HOURGLASS NEBULA

The Hourglass Nebula (above) is an example of a planetary nebula: a bubble of gas thrown out by a dying star. While some planetary nebula are round, the Hourglass has an odd shape, perhaps because its star has an unusual stellar wind.

## PENCIL NEBULA

The Pencil Nebula is a part of the Vela supernova remnant. It appears as a long, thin band, like a pencil in the sky. It is moving at about 644,000km/h. It was formed by a supernova about 12,000 years ago and is about 800 light years away.

## ORION NEBULA

The Orion Nebula (above) is one of the easiest to see and is a greatly photographed object in the night sky. It is about 24 light years across. In it, new stars and a planet are forming from collapsing areas, just as the Sun and the Earth did.

# The Milky Way

On a clear night with no Moon, you might see a fuzzy band stretching across the sky. This band is called the Milky Way. Through a telescope, it can be seen as millions of stars.

The whole Milky Way, also known as the Galaxy, contains about 200 billion stars. It is a flattish disc about 100,000 light years across.

## Spiral arms

The Milky Way has several bright spiral arms. They are bright because they contain many young stars that send out lots of light.

## Discovering the Milky Way

Although some ancient Greeks thought that the Milky Way might be made of stars, this was not proved until Galileo Galilei looked at it through a telescope for the first time, in 1610. In 1785, William Herschel made a map of our galaxy and decided that the Earth was not far from its centre. We now know that his map showed only a very small part of the Milky Way. It was only in the 1920s that all astronomers agreed that the Milky Way is just one of many galaxies.

## The Magellanic Clouds

In the night skies of the Southern Hemisphere, there are two patches of light that look similar to the Milky Way. They are small galaxies called the Large and Small Magellanic Clouds. The gravity of the Milky Way has given them twisted shapes.

## Where are we?

The Solar System is close to the inner edge of the Orion Arm of the Milky Way. It is about halfway (25,000 light years) from the centre of the Milky Way. The Solar System is moving around the Milky Way at the very high speed of around 200km/s. Even so, because it has to travel the enormous distance of 160,000 light years, it takes about 240 million years to go round just once. The Sun and some nearby stars are inside an area called the 'Local Bubble', where the gas that is found throughout the Milky Way is unusually thin.

## The view from Earth

The Milky Way is easier to see from the Southern Hemisphere because from there we are looking towards the bright centre of the Galaxy. The darker patches within the Milky Way are dusty areas.

**MEDIA**

**GALACTIC EMPIRES:** *War in the Milky Way*
The *Star Trek* series of television programs and films follows the interstellar adventures of the exploration vessel the starship *Enterprise*. Here the USS *Enterprise* (shown above) prevents war breaking out in the Milky Way between two galactic enemies, the Federation and the Klingon Empire.

# Galaxies

There are billions of galaxies scattered far and wide through the known Universe. Each is held together by gravity and contains many stars.

Galaxies may contain trillions of stars. Most are small and irregular in shape. It is not certain why this is, nor exactly how galaxies form.

## Types of galaxies

There are four types of galaxies, each with a different shape. Some galaxies have no obvious shape (1) and are called irregulars. Elliptical galaxies are shaped like flattened or squashed balls (2). Spiral galaxies have curved arms. The Milky Way is a spiral galaxy, and probably has a bar of stars in the middle (3). Some spiral galaxies do not have bars (4).

## A spiral galaxy

This a face-on view of the Whirlpool Galaxy. It is a typical spiral galaxy, with a bright central bulge and spiralling arms of stars. The galaxy is constantly spinning, forming a pattern similar to a whirlpool or water spiralling down a plug hole. The bulge is a dense mass of old stars. The whispery arms are areas rich in young stars and glowing gas. Galaxies like this one are quite rare.

## Colliding galaxies

These two galaxies are called the Mice. They have strange shapes because they are in the process of colliding. The gravity of each galaxy pulls the other out of shape, and also causes the birth of hundreds of new stars.

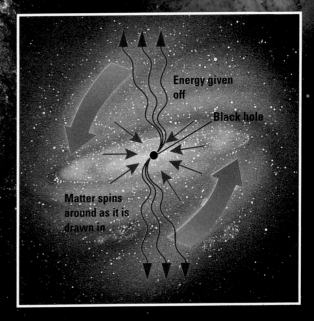

Energy given off

Black hole

Matter spins around as it is drawn in

## Active galaxies

Active galaxies contain enormous black holes. Matter falling into the holes sends out huge amounts of radiation (above). Active galaxies look very different depending on the angle we see them from. If we see them between face-on and edge-on, they are called quasars. Quasars are among the brightest and most distant light sources we know.

# THE UNIVERSE

THE UNIVERSE IS EVERYTHING THAT EXISTS. WE DO NOT KNOW HOW LARGE THE UNIVERSE IS, BECAUSE WE CAN ONLY SEE AS FAR AS A FEW BILLION LIGHT YEARS. THIS AREA IS CALLED THE KNOWN UNIVERSE. MOST OF IT IS COLD AND EMPTY.

## BEYOND THE STARS

If you could travel out from the Earth at an amazing speed, you would soon leave the Moon behind, and then all the planets. You would pass many stars, but eventually these would thin out, because you would have left the Milky Way Galaxy. Outside it, you would see many other galaxies, clustered together in groups of many sizes (called clusters and superclusters). Travelling even farther, you would see that these clusters and superclusters form long strands (called filaments) with empty spaces between them.

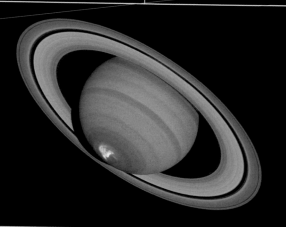

**Milky Way**
**Our galaxy, the Milky Way, is about 100,000 light years across and more than 2,000 light years thick.**

**Earth and Moon**
**The Moon is Earth's closest neighbour. It is about 1.3 light seconds away.**

**Planets in the Solar System**
**The distance from the Sun to Neptune is about 4.2 light hours. The outer edge of the Oort Cloud may be over one light year away.**

# AN ENDLESS SPACE

The Universe has no centre, and no edges either. It is not known if the Universe is infinite (goes on forever) or finite (limited in volume). Even if it is finite, you could never reach an end of the Universe. This is a bit like the Earth: Although you could travel on it forever without reaching an end, it only has a limited area to explore.

**Local Group**
The Milky Way is part of the 'Local Group' of galaxies. There are about 30 others, most much smaller than the Milky Way. This is the Andromeda Galaxy, M31.

**Distant galaxies**
Many galaxies can be seen here. Galaxies are found in clusters – like the Local Group – which are themselves grouped into superclusters. Groups of superclusters form vast filaments with enormous empty regions between them.

# The Big Bang

Following a huge burst of energy, every group of galaxies is moving away from our Local Group. The farthest groups of galaxies are moving more quickly than those closer to us.

Ever since the Universe began, it has been expanding at an incredible speed. It was formed 13.7 billion years ago, in a sudden burst of energy called the Big Bang.

## Cosmic background radiation

Although the idea of the Big Bang was suggested in 1925, many astronomers doubted it until the leftover heat radiation from the Big Bang was measured in 1964. This is called cosmic microwave background radiation. Measurements of variations in the radiation allow astronomers to trace the beginning of galaxies in the early Universe.

## The Big Bang

The Big Bang was the beginning of everything – even time and space. It was a sudden and mysterious burst of energy and was extremely hot. Very soon after the Big Bang, there was a short period of very fast expansion called cosmic inflation. Since then, the Universe has continued to expand and cool down.

**Sudden burst of energy. At this stage, the Universe contains no matter.**

**The most simple particles start to form.**

**The Universe contains quarks and gluons.**

**Quarks and gluons form larger particles.**

**Background radiation map of the sky.**

**Blue areas are high in radiation; yellow areas are low in radiation.**

The Big Bang was so hot that matter could not exist at first. But as it cooled, tiny particles formed and joined together to make atoms. Eventually, the atoms became part of stars and planets.

Particles begin to stick together.

Electrons have now joined with nuclei to form atoms.

The atoms have formed molecules, stars and planets.

Protons and neutrons have formed the nuclei of atoms, but it is still too hot for electrons to stick to them.

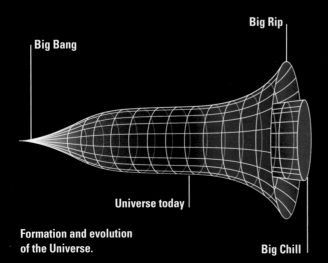

Big Rip

Big Bang

Universe today

Formation and evolution of the Universe.

Big Chill

## The end of everything

There are two main theories about how the Universe will end. According to one, the Universe will go on expanding but will gradually slow down. As it does, the stars will run out of fuel and die. Eventually the whole Universe will be cold, dark and dead. This is sometimes called the Big Chill. Or, it may be that the Universe will expand faster and faster, and everything in it will be torn apart. This theory is sometimes called the Big Rip. However, there are no signs of it ending just yet.

# Space distances

One of the most difficult and important parts of astronomy is finding out how large the Universe is and how far away the things in it are from one another. There are different methods of measurement for different types of object.

### SOLAR SYSTEM DISTANCES

The distance to the Moon is measured by bouncing laser beams off it and timing how long it takes them to come back. This is about 2.6 seconds, which means that the Moon is about 1.3 light seconds away. The same method is used to measure the distances to the planets, except that radio waves are used instead of light. This is how we know that Venus, the nearest planet to us, is about 40 million km (about 2.2 light minutes) away at its closest. Planetary distances are also often measured in astronomical units: the Earth is about one astronomical unit from the Sun.

### STAR DISTANCES

Starlight takes years to reach the Earth. We can measure the huge distances to the nearest stars because we can see them move very slightly against the background stars. This is similar to the way in which you see a tree move against a background as you go past it in a car. For more distant stars, astronomers work out the true brightness from their knowledge of stars of that type. They then compare it with the brightness of the star in the sky to work out the distance. Distances from stars are measured in parsecs: one parsec is 3.26 light years.

### GALACTIC DISTANCES

Galaxies are light centuries away. They contain variable stars, such as the Cepheids, and the brightnesses and distances of these can be worked out by measuring how fast they change brightness. More distant galaxies can be studied by working out their true sizes from their shapes and comparing this with their apparent sizes to work out how far away they are. Also, as we know that distant galaxies are moving away from us, we can work out their distances from their speeds. Distances to galaxies are often measured in megaparsecs: a megaparsec is one million parsecs.

**A distant nebula**

WEBSITES ON SPACE AND TIME

*http://hubblesite.org/explore_astronomy/way_out*   Test your knowledge of the Universe.
*http://resources.schoolscience.co.uk/STFC/bang/bang.htm*   Travel in time to and from the Big Bang.
*http://snap.lbl.gov/multimedia/animations*   Animations of the Big Bang and expanding Universe.
*http://spaceplace.nasa.gov/en/kids/blackhole*   Facts, information and a game about black holes.
*www.esa.int/esaKIDSen/Starsandgalaxies.html*   Information about stars and the Milky Way.

# SPACE EXPLORATION

The exploration of space is a vast project, and we are still at the very beginning of it. The only other world people have travelled to is the Moon. However, space probes have visited every planet and many other objects in the Solar System. Space travel needs the best technology, and relies on many countries working together.

# Space pioneers

People have dreamed of travelling into space for centuries. Usually the Moon has been their destination. In fact, almost as soon as it was realized that the Moon was another world, people talked about going there.

None of the writers who dreamed of going to the Moon came up with a practical way of getting there, but their stories did encourage scientists to think about how real spacecraft might work.

### Early tales

The earliest story of a journey to the Moon was by a giant waterspout, thought up by a Greek writer called Lucian of Samosata more than 2,000 years ago. He called his story *True History* as a joke, because he knew no one would believe it. In it, the waterspout carries a sailing ship to the Moon, whose inhabitants are at war with the Kingdom of the Sun over the possession of Venus, known as the 'Morning Star'.

### Flying through space

In 1638, the Bishop of Hereford wrote a book called *The Man in the Moone*, in which a flock of geese carry a chair – and an astronaut – to the Moon.

## First flight

Robert Goddard (1882–1945) was an American engineer who spent many years working out the mathematics of rocket flight. In 1926 he launched the world's first liquid-fuelled rocket. Although it only flew for 2.5 seconds, the idea was so good that all later spacecraft were based on it.

## Konstantin Tsiolkovsky

Russian engineer Konstantin Tsiolkovsky (1857–1935) was fascinated by the idea of space travel but had little money to carry out experiments. Instead, he worked out many of the basic ideas of space flight and suggested many things that were built decades later, from step rockets (p.101) to space stations (pp.120–121). He also worked out the speed and fuel a rocket needs in order to escape from Earth.

**MEDIA**

**FIRST MEN IN THE MOON**

In 1901, HG Wells wrote *The First Men in the Moon*. In it, an inventor discovers a metal that cuts off gravity, and uses it to build a spacecraft. He and a friend travel deep inside the Moon which turns out to be inhabited and provided with air. The image above is from a 1960 film of the story.

# Escaping gravity

To travel through space a craft must first escape from Earth, which means overcoming the force of gravity. To do this, the craft must travel upwards extremely fast and the only way we know to do that is to use rocket power.

Rockets fly very differently to planes. Planes rely on air flowing over their wings to lift off the ground and to stay up. For rockets, air causes friction and slows them down: they fly best in the vacuum (airless emptiness) of space.

**ESCAPE VELOCITIES**
The escape velocity of a rocket depends on the pull of a planet's gravity. This is why the *Apollo* astronauts needed a huge rocket to blast off the Earth, with its strong gravity, but a tiny one to escape from the Moon, which has much weaker gravity. These escape velocities are in units of km/s.

| | |
|---|---|
| Asteroid Vesta: | 0.3 |
| Moon: | 2.4 |
| Mars: | 5.0 |
| Earth: | 11.2 |
| Sun: | 617.5 |

### How rockets move
By allowing the gases produced from burning fuel to escape through the back of the rocket's combustion chamber, a forward force called thrust is created.

### Escape velocity
The harder you throw a stone upwards, the higher it gets before falling. If you could throw it hard enough, it would never come down again but continue into space. The speed necessary for this is the escape velocity.

## Step rockets

Fuel is heavy and so are fuel tanks. Both add to the weight of a spacecraft. The heavier a spacecraft is, the more fuel it needs to escape the Earth. So, as rockets use up their fuel, they discard the empty tanks, step-by-step. For this reason, these rockets are called step rockets.

Launch escape system

Command and service modules

Lunar module

Liquid hydrogen

Liquid oxygen

Liquid hydrogen

Liquid oxygen

Liquid oxygen

Kerosene fuel

Third stage

Interstage

Second stage

Interstage

First stage

Rocket fuel and *Apollo* modules

Rocket stages

**Left: A *Saturn V* rocket discards its first stage on its way to the Moon. The inside of the rocket, and its stages, are shown right.**

## Orbital velocity

It is not necessary to completely escape from the Earth's gravity if a spacecraft needs only to reach the Moon, or to go into orbit. In fact, no rocket carrying people has ever reached escape velocity. The velocity needed to reach orbit and stay there is known as the orbital velocity. It depends on the size of the orbit, but for Earth it is around 7km/s.

# Travelling through space

Almost all the fuel carried by a spacecraft is used up within a few minutes of launch, to get it away from Earth and send it on its way.

Once it is beyond the atmosphere and going fast enough, a rocket does not need to go on firing its engines to keep moving. It will stop only if it is pulled down by the gravity of a planet or other large object.

**The first stage of the rocket consists of four boosters, each about 20m long. These burn fuel for the first two minutes of a flight, creating the lift needed to get the rocket into the air. The boosters then fall away from the rocket. As the used stages fall back to Earth, they burn up in the atmosphere.**

***SOYUZ* ROCKET**
The Russian *Soyuz* rocket is used to lift military and civilian payloads into space. It is the most frequently used launch craft in the world. Its main fuel is kerosene.

## Types of fuel
Rocket fuel is either liquid or solid. Hydrogen is a common liquid rocket fuel and powdered aluminium a solid rocket fuel. As there is no air in space, rockets need to take oxygen with them. Without it, the fuel would not burn.

**The second stage of *Soyuz* burns fuel for another two and a half minutes and then separates from the last stage.**

## Payloads

A rocket's payload is whatever it is designed to carry – such as a manned capsule or a satellite. Spacecraft are the most expensive way to travel – while a truck can easily carry its own weight, a rocket may be 40 times as heavy as its payload.

**The third stage burns fuel for another six minutes and then opens its shroud to release the payload.**

**The fourth stage delivers the payload into orbit. Here the payload is a communications satellite.**

## Slingshots

Space probes to distant parts of the Solar System use the gravity of planets to help them on their way. This is known as a gravitational slingshot effect, and it both speeds the space probes up and changes their directions.

Earth

Jupiter

Sun

## Steering a spacecraft

To steer a rocket on its way up into space, its engine nozzle can be 'gimballed', that is, pointed slightly to one side. Once in space, small rockets or compressed air jets are used to change direction.

# THE SPACE RACE

On 4 October 1957, *Sputnik 1*, the first artificial satellite, was launched by the USSR. It was the beginning of a space race between the USSR and the USA.

***Sputnik 1*** sent out a bleeping radio signal that could be heard around the world.

Gagarin in his capsule

## YURI GAGARIN

The first human in space was Yuri Gagarin, a 27-year-old Russian air force pilot. Gagarin was chosen partly because of his small size – the capsule had very little room. He went around the Earth once in his capsule, on 12 April 1961. Gagarin bailed out of the capsule on the way down, landing by parachute. He immediately became an international hero.

Cutaway of Gagarin's *Vostok 1* capsule, called *Swallow*. Only the spherical re-entry capsule of the craft returned to Earth.

# JOHN GLENN

The USA was determined to catch up with the USSR. It succeeded in putting an American called John Glenn into orbit the year after Gagarin. Glenn completed three orbits of the Earth in his capsule. He returned to space on the space shuttle 36 years later. Then aged 77, he became the world's oldest space traveller.

An *Atlas* rocket launched Glenn into space from Cape Canaveral, in Florida, USA.

Glenn's Mercury capsule was called *Friendship 7*. After a flight lasting nearly five hours, it splashed down into the Atlantic Ocean.

Gagarin's space trip began with the blast-off of the *Vostok-K* rocket from Baikonur Cosmodrome in the USSR.

# Mission to the Moon

Reaching the Moon was the final aim of the Space Race – and one of the greatest events in history. Powerful *Saturn V* rockets carried *Apollo* modules with astronauts on board.

**MOON MODULES**
The three *Apollo* astronauts in each crew travelled to the Moon's orbit and back in the Command Module (CM), with the Service Module (SM) attached. Two of the astronauts travelled between the CM and the Moon's surface in the Lunar Module (LM), given the name *Eagle*. The bottom half of *Apollo 11*'s LM was left on the Moon and the upper part returned to the other modules.

SM

CM

LM

To go to the Moon and back, each of the USA's *Apollo* Moon missions involved travelling more than 700 million km through space at record-breaking speeds.

Two stages jettisoned

Take-off

Splash down

Command Module approaches atmosphere

EARTH

Third stage and modules head for the Moon

Command Module detaches from Service Module

## Escape from Earth

Within ten minutes of launch, the first and second stages had been emptied of fuel and cast off. The third stage pushed the modules into Earth's orbit. Another burst from its engines pushed *Apollo* to the Moon.

## Many missions

*Apollo 11* was the first mission to touch down on the Moon, landing on 16 July 1969. Five other *Apollo* landings followed. To prepare the astronauts and test the equipment, a series of practice missions called *Gemini* were made first.

## Return to Earth

After the Lunar Module had visited the Moon, its upper part rejoined the Service Module and Command Module, which were joined together in lunar orbit. Leaving the Lunar Module and Service Module in space, only the Command Module returned to Earth.

**Lift-off**
At launch, the *Saturn V* burned enough fuel every ten seconds to fill a swimming pool. The force of lift-off made the astronauts nearly four times heavier than normal.

**On the Moon**
The weak lunar gravity meant that the astronauts could cope easily with the bulky spacesuits that provided them with air and protection. They hopped rather than walked.

**Splash down**
The Command Module had a special heat shield to stop it burning up as it fell through Earth's atmosphere. Parachutes slowed its fall and it splashed down in the Pacific.

Command and Service modules turn around and dock with the Lunar Module

Lunar Module ejected, leaving Command and Service modules

Lunar Module rejoins the Command and Service modules

**MOON**

The *Apollo* missions followed a set flightpath on a journey that took three days each way.

Lunar Module detaches from the Command and Service modules

Lunar Module lands

Command and Service modules orbit the Moon

## Across space

The spacecraft left the Earth's atmosphere at 38,800km/h. Gradually, it slowed down as Earth's gravity tried to pull it back – until it reached the point where the Moon's gravity became stronger, pulling it faster and faster towards the Moon. Except when the engines were firing, the astronauts on board were weightless and floated around their cabin.

## Lunar orbit and landing

Only two of the three-man crews of each *Apollo* mission landed on the Moon. The third crewman remained in orbit in the linked Command and Service modules, waiting for the others to return. The first landing was watched on TV by more than one-fifth of the world's population. They heard the now famous words, 'The *Eagle* has landed.'

# Men on the Moon

Only 12 people – all American men – have walked on the Moon, and no one has set foot there since *Apollo 17* blasted off on 19 December 1972. Partly, this is because of the enormous expense and complexity of the missions.

The Moon missions did more than win the Space Race for the USA. They also allowed many new scientific discoveries to be made and taught humans how to travel through space.

Above: Apollo Mission Control in Houston, Texas

Above: Official badge of the first Moon-landing mission

Left: Neil Armstrong's footprint

## First footsteps

Neil Armstrong was the first human to walk on the Moon, on 20 July 1969. Along with Edwin 'Buzz' Aldrin, he had landed the Lunar Module in an area called the Sea of Tranquility. Meanwhile, Michael Collins remained in orbit around the Moon.

## Moon experiments

Aldrin and Armstrong had less than two hours to explore their new world. As well as collecting rocks, they carried out several experiments on the Moon. They set up a lunar earthquake detector and a special kind of mirror. A laser beam from Earth used the mirror to measure the distance to the Moon to within 6cm.

## Lunar rover

Later Moon missions carried electric cars called lunar rovers with them, which meant that their crews could explore much larger areas of the Moon than was possible on foot. The rovers could travel at speeds of up to about 13km/h. They were left behind on the Moon.

## Precious stones

The rocks collected from the Moon were very valuable, because they helped to prove how and when the Moon formed (see p.44). Pieces were sent to many countries so that scientists could examine them.

# The space shuttle

The rockets used to reach the Moon and to put satellites into orbit were costly, and they could only be used once. It was not until the 1980s that re-usable spacecraft were developed.

**SHUTTLE FLIGHTS**
*Columbia* 28 flights, from 1981 to 2003 (destroyed)
*Challenger* 10 flights, from 1983 to 1986 (destroyed)
*Discovery* 39 flights, from 1984 to 2011
*Atlantis* 33 flights, from 1985 to 2011
*Endeavour* 25 flights, from 1992 to 2011

Each shuttle consisted of an orbiter, which carried the crew, and three fuel tanks. Six shuttles were built, although the first was not used for space travel. It was named *Enterprise* after the starship in *Star Trek*.

## A re-usable spacecraft

Except for the external tank, the shuttle was fully re-usable. The twin solid-fuel rocket boosters were discarded when their fuel ran out, but they were fitted with parachutes so they splashed down undamaged and could then be collected. The external tank burned up as it fell through the atmosphere.

**The space shuttle was launched like a rocket (below), but landed like a plane (right).**

## Return to Earth

When it had completed its mission, the orbiter was turned around and fired its engines to slow itself down. It dropped down through the atmosphere and landed at an airport, just like a plane. A parachute was used to slow the orbiter's landing.

## Shuttle disasters

In total, space shuttles made 135 spaceflights. Two of these flights were disasters – in 1986, *Challenger* exploded 73 seconds after launching, killing its crew. The explosion was caused by a fault on one of the solid-fuel rocket boosters. Due to a damaged wing, *Columbia* broke apart on its way back to Earth in 2003. Again, the whole crew was killed.

## Shuttle missions

The shuttle was designed to carry out a whole range of missions, including launching satellites and repairing them if necessary, and ferrying astronauts and material to and from *Mir* (see p.121) and the International Space Station (see pp.122–123).

Shuttle *Discovery* was used to place the Hubble Space Telescope in orbit in 1990. The telescope was lifted from the shuttle's cargo bay by a robotic arm.

Hubble Space Telescope

External fuel tank

Orbiter

Solid-fuel rocket booster

# SPACESUITS

SPACESUITS ARE VITAL PIECES OF SURVIVAL
EQUIPMENT. THERE ARE TWO MAIN TYPES:
ONE IS WORN IN SPACECRAFT DURING
LAUNCH AND RE-ENTRY AND THE OTHER
IS FOR SPACEWALKS OUTSIDE.

A TV camera and lights
are fixed next to the
astronaut's helmet.

## SPACECRAFT SUITS

Launch suits are worn to protect an astronaut in case
the cabin loses pressure or needs to be evacuated.
During the return to Earth, the suits also squeeze the
astronaut's lower body to stop blood gathering there.

The suit has 14 layers.

## SPACEWALK SUITS

Any tasks done outside a spacecraft are known as Extra
Vehicular Activities, or EVAs. EVA suits are like mini-
spaceships. They provide heat or cooling, together with
water, food and protection against dangerous radiation
and the vacuum of space. Waste gases that are
breathed out are taken up by the suit and replaced
with oxygen to breathe. A urine collector is used
when the astronaut needs to pee.

In an EVA suit, thin tubes
carry cool or warm
water around the suit to
keep the astronaut at a
comfortable temperature.

This EVA spacesuit, called the Extravehicular Mobility Unit (EMU), was designed for the space shuttle.

An EVA suit also provides radio equipment for communication, and instruments that monitor the astronaut's health.

## OUTSIDE THE SPACECRAFT

On most EVAs, astronauts are fixed to their spacecraft by tethers, and they move by pulling themselves along the craft. But sometimes they must float through empty space. To do this, they use special manoeuvring units. The units squirt jets of compressed air that push the astronaut in the opposite direction – just like mini-rockets.

Above: An astronaut uses a Manned Manoeuvring Unit (MMU) to move around freely in space.

# Living in space

The lack of gravity in spacecraft makes life very different there. Almost every aspect of life is affected, from eating and moving around, to going to the toilet and sleeping.

Below: In weightless conditions, trainee astronauts float inside a cushioned aircraft fuselage. A technician, with his feet strapped to the floor to stop him floating, holds a female astronaut horizontal.

## Training for space

Astronauts need special equipment and training. In training they can experience weightlessness for brief periods (see right) by travelling in aircraft that swoop down through the air. They also need to learn to cope with the brief increases in their weight that take place when spacecraft are launched. In orbit, or in a spacecraft that is moving without using its engines, people and other objects are almost weightless. They only experience the tiny gravity of the spaceship itself, and small forces due to changes of speed. These small effects are called microgravity.

## Life in space

In microgravity, everything floats freely, including pens that work upside-down. Liquids break into floating droplets that drift around the spacecraft, so drinks must be squeezed into the mouth from special packs. A special toilet sucks away urine and faeces. To sleep, astronauts strap themselves to the wall so they do not drift about.

## Space sickness

Many astronauts experience space sickness, which is like car sickness. Luckily, it soon wears off. Other changes in the body take longer. They include the weakening of bones and muscles, and the loss of blood cells. As the spine stretches, astronauts get a few centimetres taller, too! Their bodies return to their normal heights and blood cell counts when the astronauts return to Earth.

**Right: During exercise on a running machine, an astronaut wears a harness to keep him or her on the treadmill.**

**Below: Any food crumbs must be collected before they float away.**

## Long missions

On long missions, astronauts must cope with the mental pressure of being cooped up with the same few people. It is also vital to exercise, to stop bones and muscles from getting too weak. The longest spaceflight was made by Valeri Polyakov, who spent 437 days on the *Mir* space station.

# Satellites

Any object that goes around a planet or other object in space is a satellite. The Earth has one natural satellite, the Moon. It also has many artificial satellites, sent into orbit to do tasks.

**SATELLITE ORBITS**
Thousands of artificial satellites orbit the Earth in one of four paths through space.

**Geostationary orbit**
Satellite remains constantly over the same part of the Earth; used for weather forecasting, communication and navigation.

**Low-Earth orbit**
Satellite stays close to Earth; used for mobile phone communication systems.

**Polar orbit**
Satellite passes over the North and South poles; used for navigation and weather forecasting.

**Highly elliptical orbit**
Satellite travels in an oval orbit that takes it far from Earth at some points and close at others; used for communication.

An object dropped from high above the Earth will fall straight down towards it. But if it is moving sideways fast enough, it will keep going around the Earth instead, becoming a satellite.

## Escaping the atmosphere

A satellite must orbit at a great enough height to avoid being slowed down by the atmosphere. Satellites can orbit the Earth at any distance beyond this height. The farther out they are, the slower they travel.

Polar orbit

Low-Earth orbit

Geostationary orbit

Highly elliptical orbit

## Launch vehicles

The rockets used to launch satellites into space vary depending on how high the satellite must orbit. More powerful rockets are needed for geostationary satellites, which orbit high above the Earth, than for satellites in low-Earth orbit.

## Communicating with satellites

Satellites communicate by radio signals, which are picked up by dishes (below). Some of the signals provide the satellite's location. Other signals help create photographs or maps of the Earth, or take measurements of its features.

## Types of satellites

Satellites are used for five main things: communication (relaying TV and phone signals), navigation (such as GPS – see pp.118–119), meteorology (weather forecasting and monitoring), Earth resources monitoring (for example measuring ocean temperatures or land usage) and military work (including spying).

Geostationary weather satellite

Mapping satellite

Satellite scanning Earth for minerals

Communications satellite

Measuring ocean temperatures

Military satellite

# GLOBAL POSITIONING

A CENTURY AGO, PEOPLE USED MAPS, COMPASSES AND THE STARS TO NAVIGATE — AND IT WAS STILL EASY TO GET LOST. NOW THE GLOBAL POSITIONING SYSTEM (GPS) MAKES NAVIGATION SIMPLE.

## GPS SATELLITES

Twenty-four GPS satellites constantly send out radio signals. By knowing the time that a signal was sent from a particular satellite and the time it is received, the receiver works out the distance to that satellite. By using the distances from four satellites at once, the receiver can calculate its own position.

Cars often contain sat navs (satellite navigation systems) that use GPS positioning data as well as online maps to tell the drivers where they are and how to get to their destinations. Some can also pass on traffic reports about road hold-ups and suggest better routes.

There are six different GPS orbits, with four satellites sharing each one. At any moment, signals from at least four of them can be detected by a GPS receiver, wherever it is on the Earth.

# OTHER SYSTEMS

GPS is a US system, but there are several others, including the Global Orbiting Navigation Satellite System (GLONASS), which is Russian. Some equipment can receive signals from both GPS and GLONASS. Galileo is a global navigation satellite system currently being built by the European Union and European Space Agency.

**GLONASS satellite**

**Increasingly, GPS data are used to help air traffic controllers track aircraft.**

**A sat nav provides written and spoken directions as well as maps that show the driver where the car is.**

**GPS systems also work on hand-held communication devices such as mobile phones and tablet computers.**

# Space stations

A space station is a satellite with people on board, and so far there have been four of them: *Salyut 1* and *Mir* (both Soviet), *Skylab* (USA) and the International Space Station (see pp.122–123).

Space stations allow experiments to be carried out in microgravity conditions, and astronomical observations to be made outside the atmosphere. The effects on humans in space can also be studied there.

## Space station concept

The first space station, *Salyut 1*, was launched into orbit in 1971. Because it was in a very low orbit, there was enough atmosphere present to slow it down, so it crashed back to Earth after five months. But it was very successful and 22 cosmonauts (the Soviet term for astronaut) visited it, making up ten crews in all.

Left: *Skylab* was launched in 1973. Three crews, each with three astronauts, worked there.

## *Mir* core module

*Mir* was too large to be launched in one piece so it was sent up in stages. The core module was launched in 1986 and it could house up to six cosmonauts. It remained in orbit for over 15 years and made more than 76,000 Earth orbits.

## *Skylab*

*Skylab* was made partly from pieces of leftover *Apollo* spacecraft – its largest segment was made from the third stage of a *Saturn V* rocket. Its heat shield was torn off on its way to orbit, so astronauts had to build a new one to protect *Skylab* from the Sun's heat.

## Fitting *Mir* together

Over the next ten years, five modules were added to *Mir,* together with a special attachment to allow space shuttles to dock there. Special robotic *Progress* spacecraft ferried supplies to *Mir,* while crews arrived both by *Soyuz* craft and space shuttle.

**A BRICK-BUILT HOME IN SPACE**

Space stations were written about in stories long before there were any in orbit. The first one, made of bricks, was described in an 1869 story by Edward Everett Hale (above). The space station was thrown into orbit by a huge spinning wheel.

# SPACE LABORATORY

THE INTERNATIONAL SPACE STATION (ISS) IS A SCIENCE LABORATORY BEING BUILT IN ORBIT BY 16 NATIONS. IT IS SO LARGE THAT IT CAN EASILY BE SEEN BY THE NAKED EYE FROM EARTH.

The ISS is made from modules from the USA, Europe, Russia and Japan, all fixed to a metal structure. The first module arrived in 1998 and the ISS has had people on board every day since 2000. Crews have travelled to the ISS by Russian *Soyuz* craft and by US space shuttles.

The ISS has huge solar panels that make electricity from sunlight. It takes 90 minutes to orbit the Earth and for 35 of those minutes, the Sun is hidden by the Earth. While the Sun is hidden, the ISS runs on batteries. They are recharged when the Sun appears again.

## SCIENCE IN SPACE

The ISS crews carry out experiments in many different areas, from space medicine and biology to weather forecasting and astronomy. On the ISS, the effects of microgravity on plant growth have been studied (see above).

## WORKING IN SPACE

The crew usually work ten hours each weekday, and five on Saturdays. On the ISS, the Sun rises and sets 16 times every 24 hours. But the crew stick to the same day and night periods as on Earth, sleeping for eight out of every 24 hours. There are soundproofed compartments for them, with sleeping bags fixed to the walls.

# Space probes

A space probe is a robotic machine sent to explore another planet or some other object in space. More than 100 have been launched. Probes have reached all the planets, many moons and several comets and asteroids.

Probes have many advantages over human explorers. They do not need much protection on their journeys, nor supplies of air or food. Also, they usually do not return to Earth, which saves a great deal of fuel.

## Grand Tour

In the late 20th century, the giant planets Jupiter, Saturn, Uranus and Neptune were all in roughly the same direction from Earth, so *Voyager 2* was able to visit them all. This mission was known as the Grand Tour.

**TYPES OF PROBE**

**Fly-by** probes pass close to the objects they study, taking photographs and making measurements as they pass.

**Orbiters** go around an object, collecting data over a long time.

**Landers** visit the surfaces of planets or moons but cannot move around on them.

**Rovers** crawl over the surfaces of other planets to study them.

**Sample return probes** collect material from their destinations and send it back to Earth.

**Below: The *Voyager 2* probe, which visited the four outer planets of the Solar System.**

## Fly-by missions and orbiters

Fly-by missions are the simplest and earliest sort of probe. They are the only kind that has explored Uranus and Neptune. Orbiters have visited Mercury, Venus, Mars, Jupiter and Saturn, as well as asteroids, the Moon and the Sun.

## Venus multiprobe

The *Pioneer* Venus Multiprobe sent four probes into the atmosphere of Venus in 1978. Each went to a different part of the planet. The probes were released from a 'bus' that also fell through the atmosphere and made measurements of it on the way down.

### Giotto

*Giotto* flew by Halley's Comet (see p.63) in 1986. It was named after the painter Giotto, because he painted the comet in 1301. *Giotto* was expected to be destroyed by its visit so close to the comet. It was battered by high-speed dust particles that damaged it and sent it off course, but it survived to visit another comet called Grigg–Skjellerup in 1992.

## Probe to Mercury

*BepiColombo* is a double probe that is scheduled to reach Mercury in 2019. One probe will map the planet and the other will study its magnetic field. *BepiColombo* will use a type of drive called solar electric propulsion, which is weaker than a rocket but works for years rather than minutes. It uses solar power to provide thrust.

# Landers and rovers

Landers have touched down on Venus, the Moon, Mars, Titan and an asteroid. One comet has been visited by a special type of lander, an impactor. This crashed into the comet, throwing up debris that astronomers examined.

Rovers are the most complicated probes of all, and have only been used on the Moon and Mars. The Mars rovers had to make some decisions for themselves, because it took too long for radio instructions to travel to them from Earth.

**ROVER FACTS**
The dates refer to the touch-downs.

**Moon**
*Lunokhod 1* (Soviet), Sea of Rains, 17 November 1970

*Lunokhod 2* (Soviet), Sea of Serenity, 15 January 1973

**Mars**
*Sojourner* (USA), Golden Plain, in the Ares Valley, 4 July 1997

*Spirit* (USA), Gusev Crater, 3 January 2004

*Opportunity* (USA), Meridian Plain, 24 January 2004

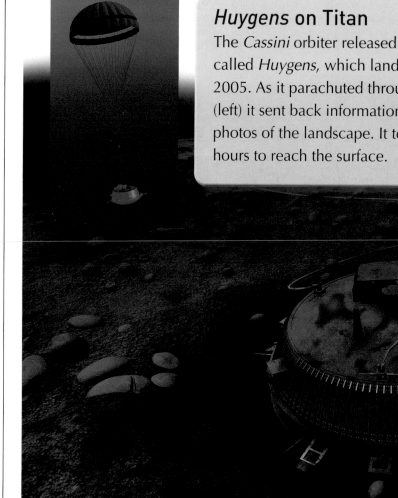

## *Huygens* on Titan

The *Cassini* orbiter released a car-sized lander called *Huygens*, which landed on Titan in 2005. As it parachuted through the atmosphere (left) it sent back information about it and took photos of the landscape. It took more than two hours to reach the surface.

## Sojourner

Parachutes, rockets and airbags were all used to make sure *Sojourner* landed safely on Mars. The rover was fitted with a special device called an Alpha Proton X-Ray Spectrometer, which was used to find out exactly what the soil on Mars was made of.

## Lunokhod *1* and *2*

Although the Americans put the first men on the Moon, the first robots to arrive there were Soviet. They were called *Lunokhod 1* and *2*, and they worked during the lunar day, powered by sunlight. The *Lunokhods* carried many instruments and measuring devices, including TV cameras. They also had special systems to ensure they stopped automatically when in danger of falling over or overheating.

## ExoMars

*ExoMars* is planned for launch in 2018. It is an advanced rover with the ability to drill down 2m from the surface of Mars to take samples. It will analyze them in its own laboratory to search for traces of life. *ExoMars* will be able to work out its own routes across Mars by taking photos of its surroundings and using them to make 3D maps. The journey to Mars will take about nine months, and a parachute will be used to slow down *ExoMars'* descent to the surface.

# Exploration timeline

Long before the first spacecraft was built, scientists had worked out the maths they needed to make it happen. In the few decades that have passed since then, spacecraft have travelled through the whole Solar System.

**1687** Sir Isaac Newton publishes his third law of motion: 'To every action there is an equal and opposite reaction.' It is the most important law of space travel.

**1883** Konstantin Tsiolkovsky publishes his theory on space rockets.

**1926** Robert Goddard launches the world's first liquid-fuelled rocket.

**1957** *Sputnik 1*, the first artificial satellite, tests out spaceflight.

**1957** The first living creature – a dog called Laika – is sent into orbit aboard *Sputnik 2*.

**1959** *Luna 1* is launched, the first spacecraft to approach the Moon.

**1959** *Luna 2* becomes the first artificial object to reach the Moon.

**1960** *TIROS-1*, the first weather satellite, is launched into space.

**1961** Russian Yuri Gagarin becomes the first human in space.

**1961** JF Kennedy, US President, talks of a plan to reach the Moon by 1970.

**1962** *Mariner 2* flies by Venus. It is the first probe to reach another planet.

**1963** Russian Valentina Tereshkova becomes the first woman in space.

**1964** The first three-person spacecraft, *Voskhod 1*, to test out living in space.

**1965** Russian Alexei Leonov becomes the first person to walk in space.

**1966** *Luna 9*, the first lander, arrives on the Moon.

**1969** *Apollo 11* mission takes humans onto the Moon for the first time.

**1970** The first rover, *Lunokhod 1*, explores the Moon.

**1971** The launch of the first space station – *Salyut 1*.

**1971** *Mariner 9* becomes the first probe to orbit another planet (Mars).

**1972** *Pioneer 10* is launched – the first probe to the outer planets.

**1978** The first global positioning satellite is put into orbit.

**1981** The first launch of the space shuttle – *Columbia*.

**1984** The first spacewalks where astronauts are not tethered to their spacecraft.

**1998** The launch of the first part of International Space Station.

**2011** The last space shuttle flight.

**A panorama of Santa Maria Crater on Mars taken by the exploration rover *Opportunity***

WEBSITES ON SPACE TRAVEL

*www.nasa.gov/audience/forkids/kidsclub/flash/index.html*   Space games, news and pictures.

*www.spacekids.co.uk/spacehistory*   History of space travel.

*www.spacetravel.org*   Space news and history.

*www.spacewander.com*   Virtual space travel.

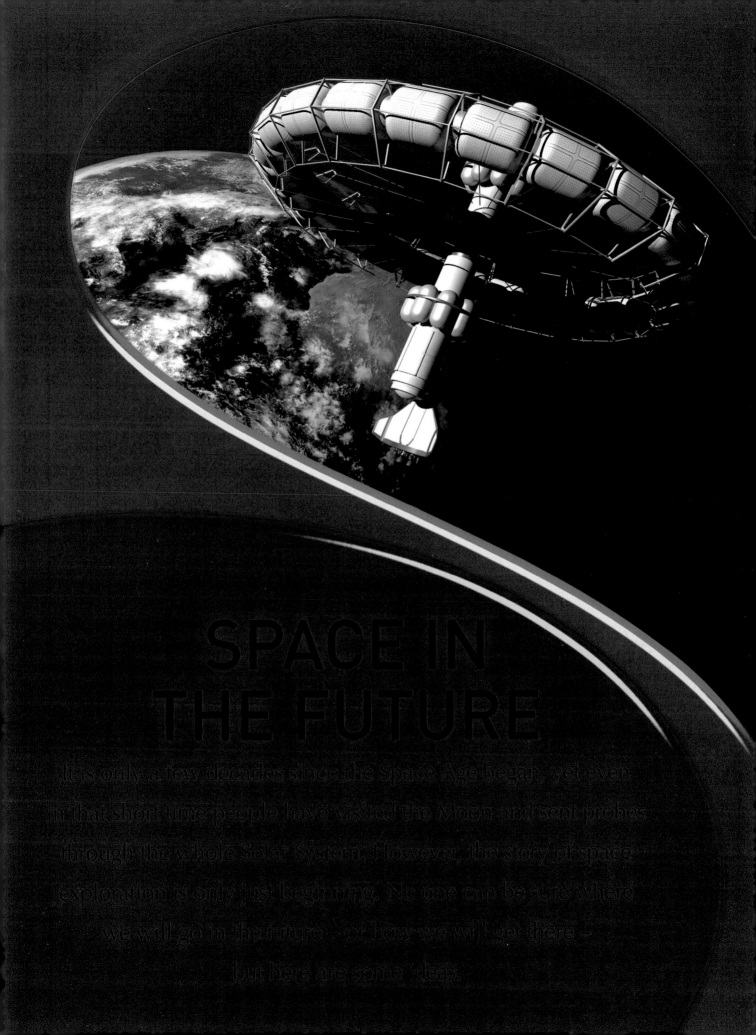

# SPACE IN THE FUTURE

It is only a few decades since the Space Age began, yet even in that short time people have visited the Moon and sent probes through the whole Solar System. However, the story of space exploration is only just beginning. No one can be sure where we will go in the future – or how we will get there – but here are some ideas.

# Spaceplanes

A spaceplane is a vehicle that can fly through the air like a plane, and also travel through space by rocket power. By far the most famous spaceplane was the space shuttle, but it was not the first, nor the last.

The space shuttle was an orbital spaceplane – that means that it was designed to reach a great enough height to go into orbit around Earth. Its last flight was in July 2011. Suborbital spaceplanes do not need to fly so high.

### First spaceplane

The first spaceplane was the *X-15* – a suborbital craft. A B-52 bomber carried it for the first part of its journey, and then its own rockets lifted it up into space.

### The *VentureStar*

The *VentureStar* was intended to replace the space shuttle as a cheaper way of launching satellites than using rockets. It was a robotic craft which could carry people if required – but it was never built.

**The *X-15* after a research flight and the B-52 flying overhead**

Right: The Boeing *X-37* is an experimental American robotic orbital spaceplane. It is lifted on an *Atlas V* rocket and lands like the space shuttle. It first flew in 2010.

Above and left: *SpaceShipTwo* is a follow-up craft to *SpaceShipOne*, planned to carry passengers at a ticket price of around $200,000.

## Future concepts for spaceplanes

A new British spaceplane, *Skylon*, is being planned that would be the first ever spaceship to reach orbit without jettisoning fuel tanks on the way. *Skylon*'s engines could be used both within and beyond the atmosphere, and the spaceplane would be completely re-usable.

## SpaceShips

Though early spaceplanes were all government funded, some present and future ones are not. *SpaceShipOne* was the first successful privately funded suborbital spaceplane. It could carry two passengers as well as its pilot and was lifted up to a high altitude by a special carrier plane. It was paid for entirely by Paul Allen, an American billionaire. A new version, *SpaceShipTwo*, is due to be launched soon.

# Mission to Mars

Mars is more than 140 times as far away from Earth as the Moon. So a mission to Mars will be longer, more complex, riskier and more expensive than the *Apollo* Moon missions.

The latest plans for a trip to Mars are for the USA to launch a manned spacecraft in the 2030s. The mission would take well over a year, including many weeks on Mars.

## The mission

Robot craft would go to Mars first to test and prepare for the human landing that would follow months later. Fuel for the return journey would probably be made on Mars itself. The USA, Russia, China and the European Union have all planned spacecraft that could reach Mars.

Astronauts will use rover vehicles to move around, and solar panels to generate electricity.

## Conditions on Mars

Mars is the most similar planet to Earth in our Solar System – but it has a very thin atmosphere, and humans would need spacesuits to survive on its surface.

Above: Sunrise on Mars, as photographed by a robot lander

## Mars craft

This is an artist's impression of a spacecraft that the USA space agency, the National Aeronautics and Space Administration (NASA), designed to travel to Mars. It is shown here blasting off from the surface of the planet on its way back to Earth.

## Mars base

Astronauts on Mars, helped by robots, would need to build a base. At the base, plants and microbes would be grown inside greenhouses to provide both food and oxygen. Inside the base, the air pressure and temperature would be like those on Earth. Protection would be needed from dangerous radiation, which the atmosphere of Mars does not block.

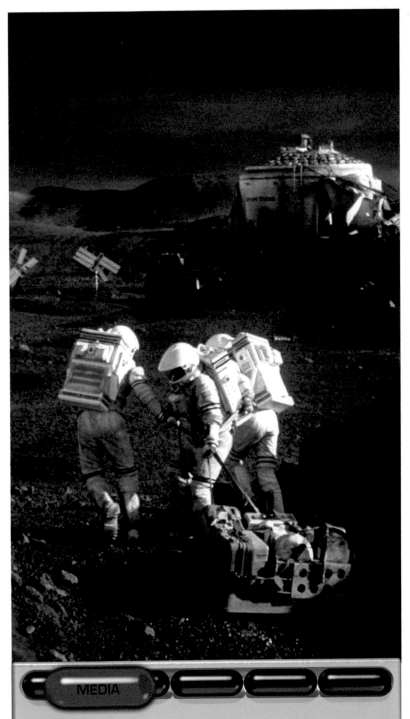

MEDIA

**MISSION TO MARS**

In the 2000 science-fiction film *Mission to Mars*, a team of astronauts and equipment are sent to the planet following a disaster during the first manned voyage there. Although conditions on Mars are harsher than those shown in the film, the problems that the rescue team encountered were real, like how to obtain food, water and oxygen.

# FUTURE SPACE DRIVES

So far, all spacecraft have relied on rocket power to leave Earth and most have used it to complete their journeys. But rocket fuel is expensive and heavy, so other methods are being investigated.

## SOLAR SAIL

The Sun constantly sends vast amounts of radiation into space. This radiation presses on everything it touches, and this pressure can be used to push large pieces of shiny material along. These are called solar sails.

**The main problem with a solar sail is that it can only be used to move away from the Sun.**

**Below: Although the push of radiation pressure on the sail is quite small, the fact that it is constant – unlike rocket power – means the sail keeps increasing in speed.**

## ION DRIVE

In an ion drive system, the outer particles, called electrons, are stripped from atoms to form ions. An electric field then squirts the ions out at high speeds, forcing the drive and spacecraft in the other direction. This type of drive has been tested on spacecraft.

**Atoms are broken down into ions and electrons.**

**Electric field accelerates ions to generate thrust.**

## NUCLEAR DRIVE

Unlike ion drives and solar sails, nuclear drive systems can create strong thrusts. The simplest type is based on nuclear fission, as used in nuclear power stations, but this creates pollution. Research is being carried out into a fusion device, which is cleaner, and releases energy as the Sun does.

## THE SPACE ELEVATOR

A geostationary satellite remains constantly 35,786km above the same point on Earth. In theory, an enormous cable could stretch from it down to the ground, and people could travel up and down it in elevators.

**Right: A nuclear-powered rocket of the future. It is streamlined to allow it to travel easily through Earth's atmosphere.**

# Mining the sky

So far, people have used space only as a place to study, or for satellites to orbit. In future, we may use it as a source of power and materials.

Using space in this way will be a great help for future space travellers, for people who remain on Earth and, one day, for those who make their homes on other planets.

## Solar power

Already, many spacecraft use solar cells to make electricity from sunlight. In future, such solar power systems may be used on groups of satellites to collect power for use on Earth. It might be sent down from orbit in the form of laser beams or microwaves.

**Right: An enormous orbiting solar power collector satellite beams energy both to Earth and to an orbital spaceplane.**

Right: Robot space-tugs pull an asteroid close to Earth to be mined, while an orbital solar array beams power to Earth.

## Asteroid mining

Many asteroids contain useful metals and other substances, and their very low gravity means that little energy is needed to ferry these materials to space destinations. The materials could also be used to build things in space, or to produce drinkable water or rocket fuel for astronauts.

## Water on the Moon

Space probes in 2009 and 2010 detected what are almost certainly thick ice layers on the Moon, close to the lunar North Pole. There are probably at least 600 million tonnes of ice there, which will be essential for future Moon bases. The ice may either have formed on the Moon, arrived on comets, or both.

MEDIA

### AVATAR

*Avatar*, a 2009 film, is set in the mid-22nd century, when humans are mining a precious mineral on Pandora, a moon of a giant star that is inhabited by human hybrids, the Na'vi tribe. Some parts of the story are very scientific – but as yet no human hybrids have been made nor have we found life on other moons or planets.

# MOONBASE

THERE ARE MANY REASONS TO SET UP A BASE ON THE MOON. THE MOON IS A SOURCE OF VALUABLE MINERALS AND METALS AND ITS LOW GRAVITY MAKES THEM EASY TO LIFT OFF. IT WOULD ALSO BE A GOOD JUMPING-OFF POINT FOR MISSIONS TO OTHER PLANETS.

## FORMS OF TRANSPORT

Astronauts use electric vehicles to travel around the Moon's surface. Manned and robot rockets and spaceplanes ferry useful metals back to Earth, and crewed spacecraft blast off for Mars.

## A NEW PERSPECTIVE ON SPACE

A moonbase with a radio telescope might be built on the far side of the Moon. Because the Earth is always below the horizon there, all radio interference from Earth would be blocked, so the observatory could study the much weaker radio signals from space.

## LIVING QUARTERS

The moonbase (below centre) acts as temporary home for the astronauts who work on the Moon. They stay at the base for a week or two before returning to Earth. The moonbase has an air-lock separating it from the lunar atmosphere to keep the air inside breatheable and at a constant temperature.

The transporter (left) carries crew from a launch pad beyond the hills to the moonbase (below).

An array of mirrors (below) direct sunlight onto a solar tower that generates electricity.

# MARS STATION

REACHING MARS IS MUCH MORE DIFFICULT THAN
GOING TO THE MOON – BUT BECAUSE THE CONDITIONS
THERE ARE MORE SIMILAR TO THOSE ON EARTH,
A COLONY MIGHT BE EASIER TO BUILD.

Right: A powerful solar-
powered radio system keeps
the colony in touch with Earth.

## CHOOSING A SITE

As Mars is a colder planet than Earth, it might
be best to create a new colony near its equator.
It might be built at least partly underground, to
protect the astronauts from dangerous solar
radiation and from extreme temperatures (both
caused by the lack of a thick atmosphere on Mars).

## TERRAFORMING

In the distant future, it may be possible to terraform, or change the conditions on, Mars to make it more like Earth. Mirrors in orbit could reflect extra sunlight on to the surface to release frozen gases there. This would thicken the atmosphere and allow liquid water to exist on the surface. Then, plants could grow and release oxygen into the air.

Below: As the gravity on Mars is low and the wind is weak, structures would not have to be as sturdy as on Earth.

## MARS BASE LIFE

Mars is so far from Earth that as much as possible would have to be produced there, rather than be sent from Earth. The thin atmosphere would make it easy to use the energy of sunlight though, and there is plenty of ice there to provide water.

# Life in space

In a few billion years, the Sun will burn up the surface of the Earth and, if humans are to survive, they must leave before then to set up homes on a distant planet or in space.

The first step to abandoning Earth will be to transport building materials to the bases. Once the bases are built, robots will be sent ahead to make living conditions suitable for people.

## Artificial gravity

The lack of gravity becomes very important on long space missions – bone and muscle weaken and blood changes, even with exercise. However, in a spinning spacecraft, the same effects as gravity are created. Things and people 'stick' to the floor, like clothes do to the inside of a spin dryer.

## Lonely journeys

Anyone who lives in space will need to take everything they have with them – the only thing available to space travellers is the power of sunlight, and that becomes weaker as the Sun is left behind.

## Space recycling

Rather than taking enormous amounts of food and air with them, large space stations could take plants instead. As well as providing food, plants release oxygen for people to breathe. They take in waste gases, too. They could even be used to make parks and gardens for the astronauts to enjoy.

## Star spheres

In the distant future, many people could live on the insides of spheres built around stars. Or, such spheres could be used to capture all the energy of a star's radiation and supply the enormous energy that spacecraft need to reach high speeds quickly. The spheres would have to be made of many separate orbiting sections.

## Generation starships

One way of reaching the stars is by a generation starship. The original large crew would live their whole lives on board, and so would their children and grandchildren, and only their distant descendants might actually reach the stars. Such craft would have to be enormous as they would be the whole world for the travellers. It would be very cut off from Earth, so the crew would have to solve their own problems and probably make their own decisions about where to end their voyage.

# Starships

It is not difficult to make an interstellar spacecraft (starship): the *Pioneer* and *Voyager* probes will eventually reach other stars. The main challenge for star travel is the time it will take to make the journey – more than a human lifetime.

Anyone travelling to another star would be very cut off from Earth. With even the nearest star, it would take more than eight years to receive a reply to a radio message. One solution for star travel is for generations of people to be born in space to survive the journey.

## Planet exploration craft

A starship would be too big to land on another world, so it would carry shuttle craft with it to journey down to the planets it reaches (below), while it either remains in orbit or continues on its way.

## Cold journeys

Small animals can be deep-frozen and then revived. This may be possible for people too, and would be another way of coping with long space journeys. Each of the small pods in this cutaway would contain a single crew member.

Deuterium  Tritium

Energy

Neutron  Helium

## Fusion power

Starlight is produced when merging atoms release energy. Similar nuclear fusion processes may be used to power starships. Merging deuterium and tritium atoms – two forms of hydrogen – produce helium and atomic particles called neutrons and release lots of usable energy.

**Left: The red section is a metal framework that uses a huge electric field to capture electrically charged space particles. This creates a reaction mass (see below left).**

## Interstellar ramjet

As well as fuel, spacecraft need 'reaction mass'. This is material that is squirted out behind them to move them forward. The interstellar ramjet (right) collects the very thin gas in space to use as reaction mass.

## Antimatter starships

Antimatter is a material that is the opposite of ordinary matter. When it comes in contact with ordinary matter, a vast amount of energy appears – more than from any other fuel and enough to power a huge starship. Scientists can make antimatter but only in laboratories.

# LIFE ELSEWHERE

IT IS LIKELY THAT MANY STARS HAVE PLANETS GOING AROUND THEM — THE FIRST SUCH EXOPLANET WAS FOUND IN 1992, AND MORE THAN 400 OTHERS HAVE SINCE BEEN DISCOVERED. IT IS VERY LIKELY THAT MANY EXOPLANETS ARE SIMILAR ENOUGH TO EARTH FOR LIFE TO HAVE EVOLVED THERE.

## WHAT ARE ALIENS LIKE?

As yet, no life forms have been found on other planets. If they do exist, it is almost certain they have evolved to fit into the conditions they live in, but we have no idea what they would look like. They might look as different as an eagle does to an oak tree. Some might be much cleverer than we are, or be bigger and stronger.

## A WORLD IN THE CLOUDS

On Earth, living things exist in boiling water, icy seas and high in the sky. Alien life forms might survive in equally harsh environments. The above picture shows the possible inhabitants of a thick, warm atmosphere surrounding a distant planet.

## WATER WORLD

Deep under Earth's oceans there are living things that rely on volcanic activity for the energy they need. There are moons in our Solar System with heat sources under their frozen surfaces too, and there may be many other worlds like this in space – with their own populations of living things.

In this imaginary image, a spacecraft has landed on an ice-covered world and sent a robot explorer to melt its way through to explore the ocean beneath.

The creatures here might communicate and hunt by using patterns of lights that are made by chemicals in their bodies.

# In touch with aliens

For a long time, people have looked up at the night sky and wondered, 'Are we alone in the Universe?' Though most people think we are not, no good evidence of alien life has yet been found.

Scientists have been listening for radio signals from other civilizations for many years, and some have sent signals out into space, too.

## Visitors from space

Perhaps one day an alien spacecraft will visit the Earth, as has happened in many science-fiction films. An alien spacecraft may not look the same as ours and could be powered differently.

## UFOs

Unexplained lights in the sky are called Unidentified Flying Objects (UFOs), but there is no evidence that they are actually alien spacecraft. In 1995 an untitled hoax film was released that was supposed to show alien corpses being studied.

**Left: This imaginary spacecraft is sending a small shuttle craft down from orbit to explore the Earth.**

## Listening for life

Many radio telescopes have been used to listen for signals from aliens, including this one in Arecibo, Mexico. Projects like these are called SETI (Search for Extra-Terrestrial Intelligence). The most interesting result so far happened in 1977 when a sudden burst of radio waves was picked up by Ohio State University's Big Ear telescope. It is called the Wow! signal because that is what the observer wrote on the telescope print-out. No one has been able to explain the radio waves properly.

## Pioneer plaques

In tens of thousands of years, the *Pioneer* and *Voyager* probes will pass close to other star systems. The *Pioneer* craft carry plaques (above) with messages to any aliens that might encounter them, showing where the Earth is. Pictures of people are shown, too. The *Voyager* probes carry gold discs containing pictures and sounds from Earth.

MEDIA

### *INDEPENDENCE DAY*

In the 1996 science-fiction film *Independence Day*, the human population is threatened by an alien invasion. Here, the alien spacecraft flies over New York City in the United States. Humans make a successful counter-attack on July 4 – US Independence Day. The film is one of the most successful disaster movies ever produced.

# Beyond time and space

In 1905, Albert Einstein published a paper showing that time flows at different rates for people moving at different speeds, rather than ticking away steadily in the background.

The discovery that time is not a constant revolutionized physics. Within a few years Einstein had shown that gravity can also change the way time flows. Using his theories, astronomers have been able to explain many of the strange objects they can see in space.

## Warps in spacetime

Massive objects warp (bend) the spacetime around them and the more concentrated their mass is, the greater the warping effect. This is why the shapes of distant galaxies can look strange: their light is distorted because it passes through the warped spacetime surrounding massive objects on its way to Earth.

## Spacetime

One of Einstein's key discoveries was that space and time are really different ways of looking at the same thing, called spacetime. The way gravity works can be explained in terms of spacetime.

### EINSTEIN

Albert Einstein, born in 1875, changed many areas of science. He developed a new area of physics, called relativity, which offered a new explanation of space, time, matter and energy. Einstein used relativity to develop the first mathematical theory of the whole Universe and to work out the most famous equation in the world, $E=mc^2$, where E = energy, m = mass, c = the speed of light. It shows that matter can appear as vast amounts of energy. It led to the development of nuclear power and nuclear weapons.

## Wormholes

Einstein's theories predict the possibility of 'tunnels' through spacetime called wormholes. If they exist, they must be tiny, but it may be possible in the future to locate and expand them, making short cuts to distant places or even other times.

## Natural time machines

The usual fate of travellers who approach a black hole too closely is to be crushed, but if the black hole is spinning and they enter the spiral, they may travel close to it without being destroyed. Some scientists believe this would allow black holes to be used to travel through space. Whether or not the space travellers could return home to Earth is as yet unkown.

# Unanswered questions

We can reach only a tiny fraction of the Universe by spacecraft. For information about the rest, we must analyze the light and other radiation from objects in space.

It is not surprising that many questions about the Universe remain, but science has already solved many of its mysteries. One day, it will probably solve them all. Here are some current mysteries.

## Dark matter

We can work out the masses of galaxies in two ways: by measuring the effects of their gravity, or by counting the stars in them. But the answers are very different – which means that most of the mass of every galaxy is in the form of a mysterious 'dark matter' that may take the form of small stars or subatomic particles, for example.

### UNIVERSAL MYSTERIES

The biggest question about the Universe is: 'Where did it come from?' Although we understand more or less the whole history of the Universe from the Big Bang until the present, no one knows why the Big Bang itself happened.

We also do not know for sure if our Universe really is all there is. It is possible that it is just one of many Universes, but that we cannot see or get to any of the others.

**Below: The mass of these galaxies and hot gas (pink) is greater than can be explained by the number of stars present. The rest is due to dark matter.**

## Dark energy

In the late 1990s, observations and analysis of the Universe showed that it is expanding faster and faster – so something must be pushing it apart. That something is dark energy, a mysterious force that makes up about three-quarters of the Universe. It seems to be a bit like gravity, but instead of pulling, it pushes.

## Dark flow

Theories of the Universe say that the clusters of galaxies we can see should all be moving away from us, at speeds that increase with distance. Yet, as well as this motion there is also a small general 'drift', too. This mysterious dark flow might be caused by an influence from outside the known Universe.

# Further facts

Although science-fiction books and films are mainly for fun, some are based on good science, like most of the ones listed here. If you want only the facts, any of the TV series listed in the third column are a good place to start.

### BOOKS
- *From the Earth to the Moon* and *Round the Moon* by Jules Verne (1865 & 1870): The first reasonably scientific books about what a Moon voyage might be like.
- *The First Men in the Moon* by HG Wells (1901): A Moon adventure that might have been.
- *The Black Cloud* by Sir Fred Hoyle (1957): A very odd cosmic event, imagined by a top scientist.
- *Welcome to Mars* by James Blish (1967): An exciting story about a young inventor's trip to Mars.
- *Cosmic* by Frank Cottrell Boyce (2008): A fun book about an accidental space adventure.

### FILMS
- *Destination Moon* (1950): Accurate prediction of the Moon landings that took place years later.
- *The Day the Earth Stood Still* (1951): One of the best 'alien visits Earth' stories.
- *2001: A Space Odyssey* (1968): This film is still realistic and thought-provoking today.
- *Apollo 13* (1995): A fictionalized account of a real drama in space.
- *Contact* (1997): What might happen if a project to pick up alien broadcasts was successful.
- *The First Men in the Moon* (2010): The best film of the HG Wells book.

### FACTUAL TV SERIES
- *Cosmos* (1980): Written and presented by top space scientist Carl Sagan.
- *From the Earth to the Moon* (1998): TV series about the Moon landings.
- *Space Odyssey: Voyage To The Planets* (2004): Though fiction, this two-part series about a future journey of exploration of the Solar System was made as realistic as possible.
- *In the Shadow of the Moon* (2006): The story of the *Apollo* missions, by the astronauts and controllers involved.
- *Wonders of the Universe* (2011): Explores the far reaches of the Universe.

**An impression of a futuristic rocket with payload in space**

## WEBSITES ON SPACE AND TIME

*http://farah-sf.blogspot.com*   Children's books, especially science fiction.

*http://sfbook.com*   Science-fiction book reviews.

*www.best-childrens-books.com/childrens-science-fiction-books.html*   Science-fiction books.

*www.filmsite.org/sci-fifilms.html*   All about science-fiction films.

*www.imdb.com/chart/scifi*   Most popular science-fiction films.

# Glossary

**altitude**  The height of an object above the surface of the Earth or other world.

**asteroid**  A rocky body that circles the Sun. Most asteroids are found between the orbits of Mars and Jupiter. Asteroids are so small that their gravity is too weak to pull them into spherical (round) shapes.

**astronomer**  A person who studies objects in space.

**atmosphere**  The layer of gases and clouds that surround a star, planet or moon. The Earth's atmosphere is called air.

**atoms**  The tiny objects, much too small to see, of which everything is made. Atoms combine to make molecules.

**aurora**  The glow in the sky seen near the North or South Pole of the Earth or other planet.

**axis**  An imaginary line going through the centre of an object, around which it spins.

**Big Bang**  The sudden expansion with which the Universe began, according to modern theory.

**billion**  One thousand million (1,000,000,000).

**black hole**  The remains of a star that pulls in any object around it in space, even rays of light, so that it appears black.

**cabin**  The part of a vehicle in which people travel.

**celestial sphere**  The imaginary hollow sphere surrounding the Earth, which seems to turn from east to west, carrying the stars with it.

**cluster**  A group of stars, or of galaxies, held together by gravity.

**comet**  A mass of ice and dust. When a comet travels towards the Sun, the Sun's heat turns some of the ice to gas and releases some of the dust, forming two tails.

**constellation**  A grouping of stars in the sky. Usually, the stars are not really grouped together but are at different distances from Earth. They seem close only because they are in more or less the same direction from us.

**core**  The central part of a planet, star or other object.

**corona**  A very hot and deep but very low-density layer of gas around the Sun or other star.

**crater**  A deep, bowl-shaped area on the surface of a planet or other world. Craters are sometimes caused by volcanoes, but more often by the impacts of meteorites, comets or other objects.

**density**  The amount of mass in a particular volume.

**dwarf planet**  A world that is smaller than a planet but that has enough gravity to give it a roughly spherical (round) shape.

**Earth**  The planet we live on, and the third from the Sun. The only planet with a single moon and liquid oceans.

**electron**  An electrically charged particle that forms part of an atom.

**equator**  The imaginary line drawn around the middle of a star, planet or other world.

**equatorial radius**  The distance from the centre of a planet or other spherical world to its equator.

**evolve**  To develop from one type of thing to another; usually refers to living things.

**exoplanet**  A planet that orbits a star other than the Sun.

**force**  A push or pull.

**galaxy**  A collection of millions, billions or trillions of stars, held together by gravity.

**gamma rays**  The most powerful type of radiation.

**gravity**  The force with which every object pulls on every other object.

**horizon**  The line where the sky meets the land or sea.

**infrared**  A type of radiation that can often be felt as heat.

**interstellar**  Between the stars.

**ion**  An atom with one or more electrons taken from or added to it, leaving it charged with electricity.

**jettison**  To throw away from a vehicle.

**lander**  An uncrewed or robot spacecraft that lands on another world to explore it, but which cannot move around on its surface.

**laser**  A device that makes a beam of light that is very narrow, does not spread out much as it moves, and is of exactly one colour.

**light minute**  The distance travelled by light in one minute.

**light year**  The distance travelled by light in one year.

**lunar**  To do with the Moon.

**magnetic field**  The area around a magnet (or a planet, star or other world) where magnetism can be detected.

**Mars**  The fourth planet from the Sun, the second smallest, and the one most similar to the Earth.

**mental**  To do with the mind.

**Mercury**  The closest planet to the Sun, and also the smallest.

**meteor**  A streak of light in the sky, caused by a meteoroid burning up as it falls through the Earth's atmosphere.

**meteorite**  A piece of stone or metal that reaches the Earth after falling from space.

**meteoroid**  An object drifting in space that may fall through the atmosphere to make a meteor.

**microgravity**  The tiny gravity force that is felt inside spacecraft.

**microwaves**  A powerful kind of radio wave.

**Milky Way**  The name of the galaxy of which our Solar System is a member.

**moon**  A world that orbits a planet. Also known as a natural satellite.

**navigate**  To find your way or course when travelling.

**nebula**  A misty shape in the night sky, usually containing dust and gas.

**nuclear**  To do with the nuclei (cores) of atoms.

**nuclear fission**  A process by which the nuclei of very large atoms break apart and release energy. Used in nuclear power stations and some nuclear weapons.

**nuclear fusion**  A process by which the nuclei of hydrogen atoms merge and release energy. Powers many stars and some nuclear weapons.

**orbit**  The path of one object around another in space.

**particle**  A tiny object, such as a grain of dust, an atom or an electron.

**planets**  The large worlds, often with atmospheres, which go around the Sun or another star. Some planets have moons.

**plaque**  A smooth piece of metal or other hard material, usually with words or pictures on it.

**poles** The two 'ends' of a planet, around which it spins. Magnetic poles are the two parts of a magnet or star or planet where the magnetic field is strongest.

**probe** A spacecraft with no crew on board, sent to explore the Universe.

**radar** A system in which microwaves are bounced off objects to find out about them.

**radiation** A type of energy that travels at a very high speed.

**radio waves** A type of radiation used to transmit messages and also made naturally by many objects in space.

**robot** A complicated machine that carries out a range of tasks, often ones which a human would otherwise do.

**rotation period** The time a planet, star or other object in space takes to turn around once. The rotation period of the Earth is one day.

**rover** A type of electric car used to explore the Moon, or a robot which can move around the surface of another world to explore it.

**satellite** An object, either natural or artificial (made by people) that orbits a planet or other object in space.

**solar** To do with the Sun.

**Solar System** The Sun, and all the planets and other objects that go around it.

**space** The area beyond the Earth's atmosphere.

**supernova** An enormously bright explosion, sometimes the result of the death of a star.

**temperature** A measure, in degrees, of how hot or cold something is.

**trillion** A million million (1,000,000,000,000).

**ultraviolet** A powerful type of radiation, which causes suntan and sunburn.

**Universe** Everything that exists.

**X-ray** A very powerful type of radiation that can pass through small objects.

# Index

# Acknowledgements

The Publisher would like to thank the following illustrators: Sebastian Quigley (Linden Artists)
Sam and Steve Weston (Linden Artists).

The Publisher would like to thank the following for permission to reproduce their material. Every care has been taken to trace copyright holders. However, if there have been unintentional omissions or failure to trace copyright holders, we apologise and will, if informed, endeavour to make corrections in any future edition.

top = t; bottom = b; centre = c; left = l; right = r

Pages 4 Shutterstock/Giovanni Benintende; 10 Shutterstock/Patrick Breig; 11 Shutterstock/Pi-Lens; 13 Corbis/Kennan Ward; 15l Shutterstock/Ozerov Alexander; 15r Art Archive/Superstock; 19 Shutterstock/Antonio Abrignani; 21 Shutterstock/RG Meier; 24 Science Photo Library (SPL)/ESO; 26 SPL/Martin Bond; 27tl Shutterstock/fstockfoto; 27bl Topfoto/World History Archive; 27br Kobal Collection/Columbia; 29c SPL/Tommaso Guicciardini; 29b SPL/David Parker; 45t Shutterstock/Vibrant Image Studio; 45b Shutterstock/Danshutter; 48l Corbis/Bryan Allen; 48r SPL/EAS/DLR/Fu Berlin (G. Neukem); 55tl SPL/Mark Garlick; 55cr SPL/NASA; 56 Shutterstock/Diego Barucco; 57 SPL/Julian Baum; 60bl Shutterstock/Dmitriy Kovtun; 60br Shutterstock/Jeffrey M. Frank; 60cr Getty/Image North America; 61 SPL/Tony & Daphne Hallas; 63l SPL/NASA; 63r SPL/David A. Hardy; 64 Shutterstock/dedek; 67 SPL/Kaj R. Svensson; 68 Shutterstock/Serg64; 73 Shutterstock/xfox01; 77 SPL/Mehau Kulyk; 83 SPL/Mark Garlick; 85 SPL/NOAO/Aura/NSF; 86 Shutterstock/William Attard Mccarthy; 88 SPL/ESO; 89 Kobal Collection/Paramount; 93l Shutterstock/Richard Williamson; 93c SPL; 98l Shutterstock/Zastol'skiy Victor Leonidovich; 98r Topfoto/FotoWare; 99l SPL/Detlev van Ravenswaay; 99t SPL/NASA; 99r Rex/ITV; 104 SPL/ RIA Novosti; 117 Shutterstock/Vadim Ponomarenko; 119t Shutterstock/Jirsak; 119l Shutterstock/kaczor58; 119r Shutterstock/Evgeny Vasenev; 120 SPL/RIA Novosti; 121 Topfoto/The Granger Collection; 122 Shutterstock/jean-luc; 123 SPL/NASA; 133tl Shutterstock/Jan Kaliciak; 133cl Shutterstock/Sebastian Kulitzki; 133r Kobal Collection/Touchstone; 137 Kobal Collection/ Twentieth Century-Fox; 148 Shutterstock/photoBeard; 149t Shutterstock/Israel Pabon; 149c Kobal Collection/ Twentieth Century-Fox; 152 Shutterstock/Neo Edmund; 152r SPL/NASA; 154 Shutterstock/1971yes